Korean
EVERY MAN'S
Conversation

Dr. Cho Hong-Seob Professor of Chungju Politechnic College

SAMJI BOOKS

PREFACE

Korea is a fascinating country from the standpoint of culture, history, and geography and so forth. Touring and conducting business in this country, as in other parts of the world, require communication adequate enough to enhance your appreciation of beauty both cultural and natural, to generate the interest of your customer in your products, and thus to create and/or expand your markets. Whether your purpose of visiting Korea is sightseeing or strict business or diplomacy, this handbook will provide you with the most useful phrases and expressions to suit your need to communicate efficiently and confidently.

With a special phonetic key, this book will give you

(1) an easy-to-follow pronunciation guide,

(2) a complete phonetic transcription for every word and phrase introduced,

(3) a handy glossary of basic terms and expressions characteristic of the Korean language

(4) a list of common abbreviations pertaining to business, and

(5) practical words and phrases covering a wide range of everyday topics and situations.

The publication of this handbook was made possible by support from the president of Samji Publishing Company. We express our sincerest appreciation for the kind encouragement he rendered while we were preparing the manuscript.

CONTENTS

INTRODUCTION

1. Alphabet and Pronunciation

(1) Alphabet

The Korean writing system is called hangul which is a kind of method of representing the sounds of phonemes. Contrary to what you've probably heard, the Korean language is not difficult to speak. In fact, some people believe it's simpler than other languages because it lacks some linguistic "headaches"(such as inflections, declensions, conjugations, genders, or verb tenses or moods). Just think of English verbs for a moment and you'll see what we mean. So-called regular verbs(like"talk" or "offer")have four different forms in English, and the irregular verbs(like "do", "give" or "see") have at least five possible forms. Any verb in English has five properties(person, number, tense, voice, and mood), and any one of them affects the verb making it different in form under different circumstances. The Korean language nas none of these problems. Korean grammmar consists primarily of rules for word order rather than rules for word change. Basically, the Korean alphabet consists of 14 consonants(C's) and 10 vowels(V's) which, when put together in the order of CV or CVC or CVCC, form syllables which in turn constitute vocabulary words. In this book, we have adopted McCune-Reischer system of transcription to show the utterances of Hangul in romanized letters.

Experience with another foreign language will be useful in uttering as well as responding to the Korean language. But don't worry if you haven't had such experience. This book with its several aids will be of great help to you. Remember that a little effort to make use of the language goes a long way in a foreign country. The Korean you meet will be delighted that you have tried to learn their language, and will be quite willing to help you for your needs.

Koreans are justly proud of much in their culture. And among their many achievements, they are perhaps most proud of their unique language, with its unbroken tradition spanning thousands of years.

(2) Pronunciation

The basic sounds of the Korean language are not hard to hear or to reproduce with practice. There are only a few sounds such as [v] and [f] in the Korean language those do not occur in English.

CONSONANTS

HANGUEL NOTATION	ROMANIZATION	KOREAN(ENGLISH) NOTATION
ㄱ	k, g	고구마 koguma(sweet potato)
ㄴ	n	나 na(I)
ㄷ	t, d	다리미 darimi(iron)
ㄹ	r, l	라면 ramyeon(noodle)

ㅁ	m	모자 moja(hat)
ㅂ	p, b	바지 ba-ji(pants)
ㅅ	s, sh	사람 saram(man)
ㅇ	silent letter*	아버지 abeoji(father)
ㅇ	ng	병 byeong(bottle)
ㅈ	ch, j	자동차 jadongch'a(automobile)-
ㅊ	ch'**	차례 ch'arye(order)
ㅋ	k'**	카메라 k'amera(camera)
ㅌ	t'**	타조 t'ajo(a bird)
ㅍ	p'**	파마 p'ama(perm.)
ㅎ	h	하늘 haneul(sky)

* when used as initial sound
** aspirated

In addition, there are 5 compound consonants in the Korean alphabet.

ㄲ	kk***	stressed sound of 「ㄱ」
		까망색 kkamang-saek(black)
ㄸ	tt***	stressed sound of 「ㄷ」
		떡 tteok(rice bread)
ㅃ	pp***	stressed sound of 「ㅂ」
		빵 ppang(bread)
ㅆ	ss***	stressed sound of 「ㅅ」
		쓰리꾼 sseu-rikkun(pickpockets)

ㅉ	jj***	stressed sound of 「ㅈ」
		짜장면 jjajang-myeon(Chinese noodle)

Besides basic 11 consonants and 5 compound consonants, there are 10 basic vowels.

VOWELS

HANGUEL NOTATION	ROMANIZATION	KOREAN(ENGLISH) NOTATION
아	a	아기 a-gi(child)
야	ya	야구공 ya-gu-gong(baseball)
어	eo	어머니 eomeo-ni(mother)
여	yeo	여름 yeoreum(summer)
오	o	오리 o-ri(duck)
요	yo	요구 yogu(demand)
우	u	우리 uri(we)
유	yu	유리창 yurich'ang(window)
으	eu	으뜸 eu-tteum(first)
이	i	이발 i-bal(haircut)
요	yo	요리 yo-ri

There are 11 compound vowels as following :

애	ai or ae sound as in	´a´ man
얘	yai or yae sound as in	´ya´ yam
에	e sound as in	´e´ egg
예	ye sound as in	´ye´ yellow
외	oi or oe sound as in	´we´ wet
위	ui or wi sound as in	´wee´ weed
의	eui sound as	´uoy´ in buoy
와	oa or wa sound as in	´wa´ swallow
워	ueo or weo sound as in	´wo´ wonderful
왜	oai or wae sound as in	´wa´ wax
웨	ue or we sound as in	´we´ well

2. Syllables

A syllable is a sound or a short sequence of sounds which contains one peak of sonority. The peak is usually a vowel, which is the nucleus of syllalble. An utterance contains as many syllables as there are peaks. In the Korean language, each sound makes a syllable. Examples are as the following :

1) Consonant+vowel

ㄴ + ㅏ → 나[na] I

2) Consonant + vowel + consonant

ㅇ + ㅕ + ㄴ → 연[yeon] kite

Phonetic assimilation is very common in the Korean language as it is in English. For instance, the actual spelling of the word 'apnal' meaning 'future' is 앞날. But it is pronounced as 암날(amnal) because the consonant 'ㅍ' sounds like 'ㅁ' when it preceeds a nasal consonant such as 'ㄴ'. When writing the 'hanguk' we find another phonetic change occurs between syllables where the final sound 'ㄴ'(n) of the syllable is preceeded by 'ㄱ'(g) of the next syllable. In some other cases, phonemic changes occur between symbols. That is, the actual pronunciation differs from the written letter.

3. Notational Devices

1) We use the apostrophe (') when the preceeding spelling is aspirated.

2) We often use the hyphen(-) in order to set off the stem from its affix or in order to demarcate the boundary of pronuncation clearly. That is, they are used, when necessary, to distinguish a sound between syllables, to help lengthen a sound, and to separate grammatical functions.

토요일	t'o-yo-il(Saturday)
한 국	hang-guk(another name of Korea)
아 침	a-ch'im(morning)
사 람	sa-ram(man)
정 구	cheong-gu(tennis)

남　자　　　　nam-ja(male)

3) The romanization of hangul is based on the actual sound.

e.g.

신 + 라 shin + ra → shilla
앞 + 날 ap' + nal → amnal
식 + 량 shik + ryang → shingnyang

4) Depending on the environment, sounds such as ㄱ(k, g), ㄷ(t, d), ㅂ(p, b), ㅈ(ch, j) can result in voiced sound or voiceless sound in the phrase or word. Sounds like these are romanized with two different symbols. In the initial position they are accompanied by aspiration. Thus we distinguish between 'g' and 'k', 't' and 'd', 'p' and 'b' and 'ch' and 'j'.

e.g.

① 거리　　　keo-ri(street)
　　도구　　　do-gu(tool)
② 다리미　　ta-ri-mi(iron)
　　군대　　　kun-dae(troop)
③ 전화　　　cheon-hwa(phone)
　　자전거　　cha-jeon-geo(bicycle)
④ 보리　　　po-ri(barley)
　　이불　　　i-bul(sheet)

PART I
BASIC WORDS AND PHRASES

1. What you need for your flight

Don't arrive at the airport at the last minute. Every time you fly be sure to get there an hour before your flight. If you want someone to meet you at your destination, let him know the details of your flight : your carrier, flight number, time of arrival, and the name of the Korean airport you are arriving at. Otherwise, something you've never expected may happen. He can be waiting at one airline terminal when you have arrived at another, quite a distance apart.

All foreigners must have passports. You can apply for it by mail or in person in your country. Consult your travel agency or international airline office. They will inform you about what documents you need to prepare and the proper procedures to follow. No international airline offices can issue international travel tickets without valid passports.

Visas are not required for travel to Korea with confirmed outbound tickets for a stay that does not excedd 15 days. Korean embassy or consulates issues two kinds of visa : short-term visa and long term visa.

① Those who are supposed to stay for less than 90 days need only a short-term visa.

② Those who choose to stay more than 90 days need to have a long-term visa as well as an entry permit from the Minstry of Justice.

Most hotels, restaurants, and reputable shops accept major international traveler's checks and credit cards such as Master's Card, Dynaster Club, American Express, and VISA, etc. Remember that the exchange rate on traveler's checks may be somewhat disadvantageous to you.

The expressions in this section are those you'll use again and again—they are the fundamental building blocks of conversation. They will be of great help to you when expressing your wants or needs. Besides they include some simple question forms. We suggest that you familiarize yourself with the following phrases.

Listed below are many short phrases that will be useful in many of the social situations already presented. Try to learn as many as you can and use them often as your situation requires.

(1) Frequently Used Expressions

Excuse me.

실례합니다. (to get attention)
shillye-hamnida.

미안합니다. (to apologize)
mian-hamnida.

Welcome!

환영합니다.
hwanyeonghamnida.

I'm very sorry.

매우 죄송합니다.

maeu choesonghamnida

Thank you (very much).

매우 감사합니다.

maeu gamsahamnida.

May I trouble you?

수고 좀 해 주시겠습니까?

sugo chom hae jushigesseumnikka?

Good

좋습니다.

chosseumnida.

Very good.

매우 좋습니다.

maeu chosseumnida.

Wonderful.

너무나 좋습니다.

neomuna chosseumnida.

You are welcome.
천만에요.
ch'eonmaneyo.

Don't hurry.
서두르지 마세요.
seodureuji maseyo.

No provlem.
문제없습니다.
munje eopsseumnida.

Yes.
예 or 네
ye or ne

Right.
맞습니다.
masseumnida.

No.
아닙니다.
animnida.

Sir.
선생님
seonsaengnim

Excuse me.
실례합니다.
shyillyehamnida.

Hello(by phone)
여보세요.
yeoboseyo.

Please.
어서/좀
eoseo/chom

Please say it again.
다시 말씀 좀 해주세요.
tashi malsseum jom haejuseyo.

Mr.
선생님
seonsaengnim

Miss
양
yang

Mrs.
여사
yeosa

Of course.
물론입니다.
mullon-imnida.

O. K. /Fine./All right.
좋습니다.
chosseumnida.

Maybe(possibility).
그럴겁니다.
geureolkkeomnida.

No thanks.
괜찮습니다.
kwaench'ansseumnida.

It's all right.
상관없습니다.
sanggwan eopsseumnida.

It doesn't matter.
문제없습니다.
munje eopsseumnida.

Oh, I see.
아 그렇군요.
a, keureokkun-yo.

Is that so?
그래요?
keuraeyo?

Really?(Is it true?)
정말예요?
cheongmalyeyo?

I think so.
그렇게 생각합니다.
keureok'e saenggakhamnida.

I don't think so.

그렇게 생각하지 않습니다.

keureok'e saenggakhaji ansseumnida.

Wait a minute.

잠깐만요.

chamkkanmanyo.

Yes, it is.

네 그렇습니다.

ne, geuroesseumnida.

Right away.

즉시

cheukshi.

Don't mention it.

별말씀을 다 하십니다.

pyeolmalsseumeul da hashimnida.

See you later.

나중에 또 봅시다.

najung-e tto bobshida.

How are things with you?

어떻게 지내십니까?

eoteokke jinaeshimnikka?

Pardon me.

실례합니다.

shilyehamnida.

Have a good trip.

좋은 여행이 되시기를 바랍니다.

cho-eun yeohaeng-i doishigireul baramnida.

Have a good time.

즐거운 시간 되시기 바랍니다.

jeulgeoun sigan doishigi baramnida.

That's fine.

좋습니다.

josseumnida.

It doesn't matter.

문제될 것 없습니다.

munjedoil geot eopseumnida.

That's the truth!
맞습니다.
masseumnida.

Here is my card.
제 명함입니다.
che myeongham-imnida.

Wait a moment.
잠깐만요.
chamkkanmanyo.

I think so.
저도 그렇게 생각합니다.
cheodo keureokke saenggakhamnida.

I don't think so.
저는 그렇게 생각하지 않습니다.
cheo-neun geureokke saeng-gakhaji ansseumnida.

You are right.
맞습니다.
masseumnida.

I'm worng.

제가 틀렸습니다.

chega t'eulyeosseumnida.

Happy birthday!

기쁜 생일을 맞이하시기를!

kippeun saengil-eul majihashigireul!

Please come in.

들어오세요.

teureo oseyo.

Please sit down.

앉으세요.

anjeuseyo.

Good luck.

행운을 빕니다.

haeng-un eul bimnida.

(2) Questions

When	Where
언제	어디서
enonje	eodiseo

Who	What
누가	무엇을
nuga	mueosseul

Why	How
왜	어떻게
wae	eotteo-k'e

What's this?
이것은 무엇입니까?
igeoseun mueosshimnikka?

How much is this?
이것은 얼마입니까?
igeosseun eolmaimnikka?

What's the matter with you?
왜 그러십니까?
wae geureoshimnikka?

Where's the station?

정거장이 어디에 있습니까?

cheong-geo-jang-i eodi-e isseumnikka?

How long have you been in Korea?

한국에 얼마나 있었습니까?

hangug-e eolma-na isseosseumnikka?

(3) Needs

I would like to _____.

_____하고 싶습니다.

_____ hago sipsseumnida.

I would like to eat _____.

_____을/를 먹고 싶습니다.

_____ eul/reul meokko shipsseumnida.

I want to _____.

_____하고 싶습니다.

_____ hago shippseumnida.

Could you give me _____?

_____을/를 주시겠습니까?

_____ eul/reul jushi-gesseumnikka?

I want to drink a cup of water.

물을 마시고 싶습니다.

mul—eul mashigo shipsseumnida.

I want to buy_____.

_____을/를 사고 싶습니다.

_____eul/reul sago shipsseumnida.

I need_____.

_____이/가 필요합니다.

_____i/ga p'iryohamnida.

Would you show me the way to_____?

_____로 가는 길을 알려 주시겠습니까?

_____ro ganeun gil—eul alyeo jushi—gesseumnikka?

Thank you very much.

대단히 감사합니다.

taedanhi gamsahamnida.

(4) Forms of Address

Listed below are traditional forms of address, which are extensively used.

Sir Kim

김선생님

kim seonsaengnim

Madam Lee

이여사님

i yeosa

Mrs. Go

미세스 고

misseuseu go

Miss Hong

홍양

hong-yang

Mr. Chang

장씨

chang ssi

(5) **Personal Conditions**

I'm thirsty.

저 목마른데요.

cheo mongmareundeyo.

I'm sick.

저 아픈데요

cheo ap'eundeyo.

I'm hungry.

저 배고픈데요.

cheo baegop'eundeyo.

I'm full.

저 배부릅니다.

cheo beabureumnida.

I'm tired.

저 피곤한데요.

cheo p'igonhandeyo.

I'm all right

저는 괜찮습니다.

cheoneun gwaench'anseumnida.

I'm sleepy.

저는 졸린데요.

cheo-neun jolin-deyo.

(6) Useful Nouns

Please give me a bill.

청구서 좀 주세요.

ch'eongguseo jom juseyo.

Let's make an appointment.

약속을 합시다.

yaksog-eul hapshida.

Let me know your address.

주소 좀 알려주세요.

juso jom alyeojuseyo.

Can I rent a car?

차를 빌릴 수 있습니까?

ch'a-reul bilil su isseumnikka?

Do you have a check?

수표를 가지고 있습니까?

sup'yo-reul gajigo isseumnikka?

What's the date today?

오늘은 며칠입니까?

oneul-eun myeo-ch'il imnikka?

Do you want the documents?

서류를 원하십니까?

seoryu-reul weonhashimnikka?

Where is the elevator?

승강기가 어디에 있습니까?

seungganggi-ga eodi-e isseumnikka?

This is my friend.

이 사람은 제 친구입니다.

isarameun je ch'inguimnida.

Please give me a hanger.

옷걸이 좀 주세요.

okkeol-i jom juseyo.

Here is your key.

여기 당신의 열쇠가 있습니다.

yeogi dangshin-eui yeolsoe-ga isseumnida.

Would you like to make a list?

목록을 만드시겠습니까?

mongrog-eul mandeu-shigesseumnikka?

How much is this magazine?

이 잡지는 얼마입니까?

i japjjineun eolmaimnikka?

Do you have a maid?

가정부를 두셨습니까?

kajeongbu-reul dusyeosseumnikka?

Are you the manager?

당신이 지배인입니까?

tangshin-i jibae-in imnikka?

Where is the map?

지도가 어디에 있습니까?

chido-ga eodi-e isseumnikka?

Don't make a mistake.

실수하지 마십시오.

shilsuhaji mashipshio.

Do you have some money?

돈 좀 가지고 있습니까?

don jom gajigo isseumnikka?

What is your name?

이름이 무엇입니까?

ireum-i mueoshimnikka?

Here is today's newspaper.

오늘 신문이 여기 있습니다.

oneul shinmun-i yeogi isseumnida.

Is this your office?

여기가 당신의 사무실입니까?

yeogiga dangshin-eui samushilimnikka?

Please help me bring my package.

내 소포 가져오는 것 좀 도와주세요.

nae sop'o gajyeo-o-neun geo jjom dowajuseyo.

Do you have some tissues?

휴지가 있습니까?

hyujiga isseumnikka?

We need raincoats.

비옷이 필요합니다.

pioshi pp'iryo-hamnida.

I would like to make a reservation.

예약을 하고 싶습니다.

yeyag-eul hago shipsseumnida.

Where is a Western restaurant?

양식집이 어디에 있습니까?

yangshikjib-i eodi-e isseumnikka?

Can I buy shirts here?

여기서 셔츠를 살 수 있습니까?

yeogiseo shyeoch'eu-reul sal su isseumnikka?

(7) Useful Antonyms

above/below

위에/아래에

wi-e/arae-e

ahead/behind

먼저/뒤에

meonjeo/twi-e

beautiful/ugly

아름다운/미운

areumdaun/miun

best/worst

가장좋은/가장나쁜

kajang jo-eun/

kajang nappeun

big/small

큰/작은

k'eun/chageun

dark/light

어두운/밝은

eodu-un/palgeun

delicious/bitter

달콤한/쓴

talk'omhan/sseun

early/late

일찍/늦게

iljjik/neukke

easy/difficult

쉬운/어려운

sui-un/eoryeo-un

expensive/cheap

값비싼/값싼

kabbissan/kabssan

few/many
적은/많은
cheog-eun/man-eun

first/last
처음/마지막
ch'eo-eum/majimak

front/back
앞/뒤
ap/twi

full/empty
가득찬/빈
kadeukch'an/pin

good/bad
좋은/나쁜
cho-eun/nappeun

heavy/light
무거운/가벼운
mugeo-un/kabyeo-un

hot/cold
더운/차거운
teo-un/ch'ageoun

intelligent/stupid
총명한/어리석은
ch'ongmyeonghan/eorseok-eun

inside/outside
안에/밖에
an-e/pakk-e

large/small
큰/작은
keun/chageun

more/less
더 많은/더 적은
teo-man-eun/teo cheog-eun

near/far
가까운/먼
kakka-un/meon

old/new
오랜/새로운
oraen/saeroun

strong/weak
튼튼한/약한
t'eunt'eunhan/yakhan

quiet/noisy
조용한/시끄러운
choyong-han/
shikkeu-reo-un

warm/cool
따스한/시원한
ttaseu-han/
shiweon-han

same/different
똑같은/다른
ttoggat-eun/tareun

young/old
나이어린/나이든
nai-eorin/nai deun

open/shut
열려있는/닫힌
yeolyeo-inneun/tach'in

right/wrong
옳은/그른
oreun/geureun

slow/fast
느린/빠른
neurin/ppareun

thin/thick
엷은/두꺼운
yeolbun/tukkeo-un

wide/narrow
폭이 넓은/폭이 좁은
p'ok-i neolbeun/p'ok-i jobeun

(8) Directions

north 북(puk)

west 동(tong)

at the corner 구석에서
(kuseog-eseo)

left 왼쪽 (oen-jjok)

middle 가운데 (kaunde)

south 남(nam)

west 서(seo)

straight ahead 곧장, 똑바로
(kojjang, ttokpparo)

right 오른쪽(oreun-jjok)

(9) Days, Weeks, Seasons

What day is it today?

오늘이 무슨 요일입니까?

oneur-i musseun yoil-imnikka?

It's_____.

_____요일입니다.

_____yoil-imnida.

Sunday
일요일(iryoil)

Tuesday
화요일(hwayoil)

Thursday
목요일(mogyoil)

Saturday
토요일(t'oyoil)

Monday
월요일(woryoil)

Wednesday
수요일(suyoil)

Friday
금요일(keumyoil)

today
오늘(o-neul)

yesterday
어제(eoje)

the day before yesterday
그저께(keujeo-kke)

tomorrow
내일(nae-il)

the day after tomorrow
모레(morae)

week
주(chu)

this week
금주(keumju)

last week
지난주(chinan-ju)

next week
다음주(taeum-ju)

for one week
일주일동안(iljjuil-dong-an)

for two weeks
이주일동안(ijuil-dong-an)

in one week
일주일만에(iljuil-man-e)

in the afternoon
오후에(ohu-e)

in the early evening
초저녁에(ch'ojeonyeog-e)

in the evening
저녁에(chonyeog-e)

in one day
하루만에(haru-man-e)

in two days
이틀만에(it'eul-man-e)

three days ago
사흘전(saheul-jeon)

this morning
오늘아침(oneul ach'im)

this afternoon
오늘 오후(oneul ohu)

tonight
오늘 밤(oneul ppam)

tomorrow night
내일밤(naeilppam)

in the morning
아침에(ach'im-e)

by morning
아침까지(ach'im-kkaji)

by Tuesday
화요일까지(hwayoil-kkaji)

weekday
주중(chujung)

weekend
주말(chumal)

everyday
매일(maeil)

work day
근무일(keunmuil)

per day
하루에(haru-e)

during the week
주중에(chujung-e)

a week from today on
오늘부터 일주일간
(o-neulbut'eo iljuil-gan)

spring
봄(pom)

summer
여름(yeoreum)

autumn
가을(ka-eul)

winter
겨울(kyeo-ul)

2. Phrases for Survival

You may not speak a word of Korean but, if you memorize the next set of phrases, you will be able to impress people as a person of good manners and start accumulating basic knowledge of things you encounter in a new setting. Remember that 'insa' or saying 'hi' is regarded as a very nice and important gesture when you meet someone for the first time and any time you see her or him again.

(1) Useful Expressions

I am pleased to meet you (lit. "I see you for the first time"). Let me introduce myself.

My name is_____.
저는 _____입니다.
cheoneun_____imnida.

Excuse me.
실례합니다.
shilyehamnida.

Thank you.
고맙습니다.
komapsseunminda.

See you again.
다시 뵙겠습니다.
tashi boipkkesseumnida.

Hello.
여보세요.
yeoboseyo.

Please help me.
좀 도와 주십시오.
chom dowajushipshiyo.

What's that?
저것은 무엇입니까?
cheogeosseun mueoshimnikka?

What's this?
이것은 무엇입니까?
igeosseun mueoshimnikka?

How do I get to_____?
_____는/은 어떻게 갑니까?
_____neun/eun eotteoge gamnikka?

Where is_____?
_____는/은 어디에 있습니까?
neun/eun eodi-e isseumnikka?

(2) Terms of Social Import and Miscellaneous Words

family	home
가족	가정
kajog	kajeong
parents	children
부모님	자녀/아이들
pumonim	chanyeo/aideul
son	daughter
아들	딸
adeul	ttal
father	mother
아버지	어머니
abeoji	eomeoni
grandfather	grandmother
할아버지	할머니
halabeoji	halmeoni
younger sibling/brother	elder brother
동생	형님
tongsaeng	hyeongnim
elder sister	nephew/niece
누님	조카
nunim	chok'a

homeland/hometown	friend
고향	친구
kohyang	ch'ingu
friendship	marriage
우정	결혼
ujeong	kyeolhon
school/university	student
학교/대학교	학생
hakkyo/taehakkyo	haksaeng
major	occupation
전공	직업
cheon-gong	chigeop
(old) classmate	mailing address
동문/동기	주소
tongmun/tong-gi	chuso
number	FAX
번호	홱스
peonho	hoaekseu
contact	memo
연락	메모지
yeolak	memo(ji)

pencil	pen
연필	펜
yeonp'il	pen
newspaper	newspaper company
신문	신문사
shinmun	shinmunsa
magazine	television
잡지	테레비
chapjji	t'erebi
radio	copy
라디오	복사
radio	poksa
copying machine	mom and pa store
복사기	가게
poksagi	kage
laundry	supermarket
세탁소	수퍼
set'akso	sup'eo

3. Greetings

Greetings are a way to get started in a foreign language. After all, when you arrive, you'll want to say things like "Hello, my name is⋯, what's your name?" or "Hi, I'm a tourist, can you help me find my hotel?" Phrases like these will be found in this section. You can use these expressions throughout your trip, or even with your Korean friends. Besides being applicable all the time, these basic words and phrases will also be helpful with your pronunciation because they contain many of the most common sounds in the Korean language. Try to learn as many as you can.

Korean surnames are quite simple, usually consisting of one syllable, followed by the given name (note that this is the reverse of Western practice). Titles, such as Mr. and Mrs., will always follow the name rather than preceding them. We'll see examples of this sort in the following section.

How do you do?
처음 뵙겠읍니다.
ch'eoeum boep—kesseumnida.

How are you (doing)?
안녕하세요?
annyeong—haseyo?

Good afternoon.
안녕하십니까?
annyeong-hashimnikka?

Good evening.
안녕하십니까?
annyeong-hashimnikka?

Good day.
안녕하십니까?
annyeong-hashimnikka?

Good night.
안녕히 주무세요.
annyeonghi jumuseyo.

Glad(Pleased) to see(meet) you.
만나서 반갑습니다.
mannaseo ban-gapsseumnida.

Hello.
안녕하십니까?(for greeting)
annyeong-hashimnikka?
여보세요?(for phone call)
yeobo-seyo.

Good bye!
안녕히 가세요.(to sb. leaving_____)
annyeonghi gaseyo.

See you later.
안녕히 계세요.
annyeonghi gyeseyo.

See you later.
나중에 봅시다.
najung-e bobssida.

Forget it.
잊으십시오.
ijeushipshyo.

Never mind.
걱정마십시오.
keogjjeong-mashipshyo.

This is Mr_____.
이분은 _____입니다.
ibun-eun_____imnida.

No problem.
문제없습니다.
munje-eupseumnida.

Hello, Mr. Kim?
김 선생님 안녕하세요?
Kim seonsaeng-nim annyeonghaseyo?

How are you today?
오늘은 어떠세요?
oneul-eun eotteoseyo?

Oh, I see.
아, 알겠습니다.
a, al-gesseumnida.

I'm fine, thanks.
잘 있습니다. 감사합니다.
chal isseumnida. kamsahamnida.

And you?
당신은 어떠세요?
tangshin-eun eotteoseyo?

Pretty good.
아주 좋습니다.
aju josseumnida.

Are you going shopping?
시장에 가려고 합니까?
shijang-e garyeogo hamnikka?

Yes, I am.
　네, 그렇습니다.
　ne, keureoseumnida.

It's almost time for lunch now.
　이제 점심시간이군요.
　ije jeomshim-shigan-igunyo.

See you later. (or Be seeing you)
　다시 만납시다.
　tashi man-napshida.

PART II
FOR SIGHTSEEING TRAVELERS

1. Before you leave for Korea

Don't go to Korea without any knowledge about the people you are going to meet.

It is important to know at least a little bit about the host country's culture. People everywhere like to be greeted by a foreigner in their own tongue. Do some study in advance about Korea when you are making plans to visit, not only her geography but also the socio-cultural background of the people.

(1) **Who are you?** and **Where do you come from?**

Where do you come from?

어디서 오셨습니까?

eodiseo ossyeosseumnikka?

Who are you?

당신은 누구십니까?

tangshin—eun nugushimnikka?

I am_____(your name).
저는 _____입니다.
cheo-neun_____imnida.

Where do you come from?
어디 출신이십니까?
eodi ch'ulshinishimnikka?

I come from the United States.
미국출신입니다.
migukch'ulshinimnida.

I come from England.
영국출신입니다.
yeonggukch'ulshinimnida.

I come from Canada.
카나다 출신입니다.
k'anada ch'ulshinimnida.

What nationality are you?
국적은 어디십니까?
kugjeog-eun eodishimnikka?

I am(an) American/Canadian/Englishman.
저는 미국인/카나다인/영국인입니다.
cheoneun migug-in/kanada-in/yeonggug-in-imnida.

I am(an) American/Australian.
저는 미국인/호주인입니다.
cheoneun migug-in/hojuin-imnida.

What's your full name?
성함은요?
seongham-eun yo?

My full name is John Smith
제 성명은 존 스미스입니다.
ch'e seongmyeong-eun jon seumiseu-imnida.

What's your surname(family name)?
당신의 성씨는 무엇입니까?
tangshin-eui seongssi-neun mueoshimnikka?

My surname is Kim.
제 성은 김(씨)입니다.
che seong-eun Kim(ssi)imnida.

What's your first name?
당신의 이름은 무엇입니까?
tangshin-eui ireum-eun mueoshimnikka?

My first name is John.
제 이름은 존입니다.
che ireum-eun jon-imnida.

(2) **Whose is this?** and **Where is it?**

Whose is this?
이것은 누구의 것입니까?
igeosseun nugu-eui geoshimnikka?

That's mine.
그것은 제 것입니다.
keugeosseun che geoshimnida.

It's ours.
그것은 우리들 것입니다.
keugeosseun urideul geoshimnida.

Is it yours or not?
그것이 당신의 것입니까?
keugeoshi dangshineui geoshimnikka?

Is it his?
그것이 그의 것입니까?
keugeoshi geu-eui geoshimnikka?

No, it's not. It's mine.
아닙니다. 그것은 제 것입니다.
animnida. geugeoseun chegeoshimnida.

Where is _____?
_____이 어디에 있습니까?

_____ i eodi-e isseumnikka?

Where is my luggage?
제짐은 어디에 있습니가?
che jim-eun eodi-e isseumnikka?

Where's the bathroom?
화장실은 어디에 있습니까?
hwajangshil-eun eodi-e isseumnikka?

Where's the restaurant?
식당은 어디에 있습니까?
shikttang-eun eodi-e isseumnikka?

(3) Here and There

It's here.
그것은 여기에 있습니다.
geugeosseun yeogi-e isseumnida.

It's there.
그것은 저기에 있습니다.
geugeosseun cheogi-e isseumnida.

It's on the left.
그것은 왼쪽에 있습니다.
geugeosseun oinjjog-e isseumnida.

It's on the right.
그것은 오른 쪽에 있습니다.
geugeosseun oreun jjog-e isseumnida.

(4) **What, When, Which and Why**
What is that?
저것은 무엇입니까?
cheo geosseun mueoshimnikka.

That's my luggage.
그것은 제짐입니다.
keugeosseun chejimimnida.

What do you want?
무엇을 원하십니까?
mueosseul wonhashimnikka.

I want to ask your help
당신의 도움을 청하고 싶습니다.
tangshin-eui doum-eul cheonghago shipseumnida.

When do we go?
언제 떠날까요?
eonje tteonalkkayo.

When will he come?
그가 언제 올까요?

keuga eonje olkkayo.

Which day?
무슨요일에요?
museun yoileyo.

Today.	Which year?
오늘요.	어느해에요?
oneul-yo.	eo-neu hae-eyo.

Next year.	Which way?
내년에요.	어느쪽에요?
naenyeon-e yo.	eoneujjog-yeo.

This way, please.
이쪽입니다.
ijjog-imnida.

Which one do you want?
어느 것을 원하십니까?
eoneu geosseul wonhashimnikka.

I want this one.
이것을 원합니다.
igeosseul wonhamnida.

Do you have (a) pencil?

연필(좀) 가지고 계십니까?
yeonph'il(jom) gajigo gyeshimnikka.

Yes, I have.
네 가지고 있습니다.
ne gajigo isseumnida.

No, I don't have (one).
아니요, 가지고 있지 않습니다.
aniyo, gajigo ijji anseumnida.

Why did you come?
왜 오셨습니까?
oae ossyeosseumnikka?

I've come to buy things.
물건사러 왔습니다.
mulgeonsareo oasseumnida.

(5) **Some more basic expressions**
That's correct.
맞습니다.
masseumnida.

How kind you are!
정말 친절하시군요.
cheongmal ch'injeolhashigunyo.

Mr. Lee.
미스터 리.
misteo ri.

Mrs. Kim
미세스 김
miseseu gim

Miss. Go
미스 고.
miseu go.

Do you understand?
아시겠습니까?
ashigesseumnikka.

Yes, I understand.
네, 알겠습니다.
ne algesseumnida.

I don't understand.
모르겠습니다.
moreugesseumnida.

Do you know about it?
그것에 대해 아십니까?
geugeosse daehae ashimnikka.

I know.
  압니다.
  amnida.

I don't know.
  모릅니다.
  mo-reumnida.

Terrific!
  정말 좋습니다.
  cheongmal joseumnida.

After you please.
  먼저 가세요.
  meonjeo gaseyo.

Please help me.
  도와주세요.
  dowa juseyo.

Thank you for helping me.
  도와주셔서 감사합니다.
  dowajusyeoseo kamsahamnida.

Please wait for me.
  기다려 주십시오.
  kidaryeo jushipshio.

Thank you for waiting for me.
기다려주셔서 감사합니다.
kidaryeo jushyeoseo gamsahamnida.

What a pity!
안됐군요
andoekkunyo.

Please hurry.
서두르십시오.
seodureushipshio.

Wait!
기다리십시오.
kidarishipshiyo.

Careful.
조심하세요.
choshimhaseyo.

Please say it again.
다시 말씀해 주십시오.
tashi malsseum-hae jushipshyo.

Have a good trip!
여행 재미있게 하십시오.
yeohaeng jaemiigge hashipshio.

How have you been, Mr. Lee?

이선생님 어떻게 지내셨습니까?

iseonsaeng eotteok'e jinaesyeosseumnikka?

2. When you arrive

After a long trip, you arrive at the Kimpo International Airport where customs officials await you. Passing through customs is a formality you'll want to finish quickly to start enjoying Korea. The phrases in this section are tailored to the particular set of terms and phrases used/heard around the customs inspection counter. Some customs officials in Korea speak good English, so if you have a problem, you'll be understood and helped promptly.

Your most important document during this part of your trip is the customs declaration form. On it you will itemize cameras, watches, jewelry and foreign currency taken into Korea. Keep the lists of your personal possessions, record and other reports, and currency (exchange vouchers, receipts for large purchases, and so forth).

(1) Passport Clearance

Here's my passport.

여기 제 여권이 있습니다.

yeogi je yeokkweon-i isseumnida.

My name is John.

제 이름은 죤입니다.

che ireum-eun jyon-imnida.

I'm _____.
저는 _____사람입니다.
cheo-neun _____ saram-imnida.

I'm Japan.
저는 일본사람입니다.
cheo-neun ilbon saram-imnida.

I'm Canadian
저는 카나다 사람입니다.
cheo-neun k'anada saram-imnida.

I'm British.
저는 영국사람입니다.
cheo-neun young-guk saram-imnida.

I'm Australian.
저는 호주사람입니다.
cheoneun hoju saram-imnida.

Could you tell me where the toilet is?
화장실이 어디에 있는지 말씀해 주시겠습니까?
hwajangshil-i eodi-e inneunji malsseum-hae jusige-
sseumnikka?

My address is_____.

저의 주소는 _____입니다.

cheo-eui chuso-neun _____imnida.

I'll be staying at the Hotel Lotte.

저는 롯데호텔에 머물려고 합니다.

cheo-neun lotte hotel-e meomul-lyeogo hamnida.

Here is(are) my passport.

저의 여권이 여기 있습니다.

cheo-eui yeokkwon-i yeogi-e isseumnida.

documents	passport
서류	여권
seoryu	yeogweon

health certificate	visa
건강 증명서	입국사증
keon-gang jeungmyeongseo	ibkkug sajeung

I have come_____.

저는 _____때문에 왔습니다.

cheo-neun_____ ttaemun-e oasseumnida.

on business
사업때문에
saeop-ttaemun-e
on vacation
휴가로
hyuga-ro

on a visit
방문하러
pangmun-hareo
to visit relatives.
친척을 찾아 보려고
ch'incheog-eul ch'aja boryeogo

I'm here with a group.
나는 일행이 있습니다.
na-neun ilhaeng-i isseumnida.

I'll be staying_____.
저는 _____ 머물려고 합니다.
cheo-neun _____ meomulyeogo hamnida.

a few days
며칠
myeoch'il

a few weeks
몇주
myeojju

a week
일주일
ilju-il

a month
한달
handal

alone
혼자

with my husband
남편과 함께

honja
namp'yeon–gwa hamkke

with my wife
아내와 함께
anae-wa hamkke

with my family
가족과 함께
kajokkwa hamkke

with my friend
친구와 함께
ch'in-gu-wa hamkke

with my colleague
동료와 함께
dongryo-wa hamkke

with a tour group
관광일행과 함께
k'wankwang-ilhaeng-gwa hamkke

(2) Customs

Have you anything to declare?
신고할 것이 있습니까?
shin-gohal geossi isseumnikka.

I don't have anything to declare.
신고할 것이 없습니다.
shin-gohalgeossi eopsseumnida.

I have to declare_____.
_____을 신고해야 합니다.

_____eul shin-gohaeya hamnida.

one camera	three bottles of medicine
카메라 하나	약 3병
k'amera hana	yak sebyeong
two watches	four pieces of jewelry
시계 둘	보석류 4개
shigye dul	poseongnyu negae
one carton of cigarettes	one bottle of whisky
담배 한박스	위스키 한병
tambae hanbakseu	wisk'i hanbyeong

twenty rolls of film
필름 20통
p'ileum ishipt'ong

five hundred dollars of U.S. currency
미화 500불
mihwa obaekpul

Must I pay duty on this?
이것도 세금을 물어야 합니까?
igeotto segeum-eul muleoya hamnikka?

You must pay duty on this.

이것도 세금을 물어야 합니다.

igeotto segeum-eul muleoya hamnida.

How much?

얼마나요?

eolmanayo?

These are personal articles.

이것들은 제 개인소지품입니다.

igeotteul-eun je gaein sojip'umimnida.

Please open this suitcase.

이 가방 좀 열어 주십시오.

igabang jom yeol-eo jushipshio.

Have you any more luggage?

짐이 더 있습니까?

chim-i deo isseumnikka?

This is all I have.

이것이 모두입니다.

igeossi modu-imnida.

Where can I find an interpreter?

통역원이 있습니까?

t'ong-yeok-weon-i isseumnikka?

Please speak in English.

영어로 말해 주세요.

yeong-eo-ro malhaejuseyo.

I want to make a telephone call.

전화걸고 싶습니다.

cheonhwageolgo shipsseumnida.

(3) Baggage

Excuse me, porter!

여보세요, 아저씨.

yeoboseyo, ajeossi.

Please help me with my luggage.

짐 좀 운반해주세요.

chim jom unbanhaejuseyo.

Where is your luggage?

짐이 어데 있습니까?

chim-i eodi-e isseumnikka?

This is my luggage.

이것이 제짐입니다.

igeossi je jimimnida.

Those are not mine.

이것들은 제 짐이 아닙니다.

igeotteuleun jejim-i animnida.

That is mine.

저것이 제 것입니다.

cheogeossi jegeoshimnida.

I have five pieces of _____.

저는 다섯덩이의 _____ 이 있습니다.

cheoneun daseotteong-i eui_____ i isseumnida.

big luggages	blue luggages
큰 짐들	푸른색깔의 짐들
k'eun jimdeul	p'ureun saekkal-eui jimdeul

small luggages	black luggages
작은 짐들	검은색깔의 짐들
chag-eun jimdeul	keom-eun saekkal-eui jimdeul

brown luggages
갈색의 짐들
k'alsaekeui jimdeul

Those two pieces are also mine.
이 두개의 짐도 저의 것입니다.
i-dugae-eui jimdo jeo-eui geoshimnida.

One piece is missing.
한개가 없어졌습니다.
hangae-ga eopseo-jeosseumnida.

Is it this one?
이것입니까?
igeossimnikka?

Yes, that's mine.
네 그것이 제 것입니다.
ne, keugeossi je geossimnida.

I've lost my luggage.
제 짐을 분실했습니다.
che jim-eul bunshilhaesseumnida.

Can you help me find it?

찾는데 도와주시겠습니까?

ch'anneun de dowajushigesseumnikka?

Where's the Lost and Found Office?

분실물사무실이 어디에 있습니까?

punshilmul samushil-i eodi-e isseumnikka?

Please take these bags_____.

이 짐들을 _____로 가져가세요.

i jimdeul-eul_____ro gajyeogaseyo.

outside	to the taxi stand.
밖으로	택시타는 곳으로
pakkeuro	t'aekshi-t'aneun gosseuro

inside	to the bus station.
안으로	버스 정거장으로
aneuro	beoseu jeong-geojang-euro

Where can I get a taxi?

어데서 택시를 탈 수 있습니까?

eodiseo t'aekshi-reul t'alsu isseumnikka?

Where's the bus station?

버스정거장은 어디에 있습니까?

peoseu jeonggeojang-eun eodi-e isseumnikka?

I want to go to the Shilla hotel

신라호텔로 가고 싶습니다.

shila hot'el-ro gago shipsseumnida.

Thank you for your help.

도와주셔서 감사합니다.

towajusyeoseo gamsahamnida.

(4) Transportation

taxi	car with driver
택시	운전수딸린 차
taek-shi	unjeonsu-ttalin ch'a
bus(stop)	subway(station)
버스(정거장)	지하철(역)
peoseu(jeong-geo-jang)	chihach'eol(yeok)
plane	airport
비행기	비행장
pihaeng-gi	pihaeng-jang

I'd like to go to the _____ Hotel.

저는 _____호텔에 가고 싶습니다.

cheo-neun_____ hot' el-e gago-shipseumnida.

Lotte	Chosun
롯데	조선
lot'e	choseon

Shilla	Hilton
신라	힐튼
shila	hilt'eun

Walker Hill	Sejong
워커힐	세종
weokeo-hil	sejong

Plaza	Ramada
플라자	라마다
p'eulaja	ramada

Where can I get a taxi?

어디서 택시를 탑니까?

eodiseo t'aekshi-reul tamnikka?

Please take me to this address.

이 주소로 좀 데려다 주십시오.

i juso-ro jom deryeoda jushibshiyo.

I want to go to_____.

_____에 가고 싶습니다.

_____e gago shibseumnida.

U.S. Emgbassy

미국 대사관

migug daesagwan

Namdaemun market

남대문 시장

namdaemun shijang

Canada Consulate

카나다 영사관

k'anada yeongsagwan

Australina Embassy

호주 대사관

hoju daesagwan

Stop here, at the corner, please.

여기 모퉁이에 세워주십시오.

yeogi mot'ung-i-e se-weo jushipshiyo.

Please wait for me.

좀 기다려주십시오.

chom gida-ryeo jushibshiyo.

I'll be right back.

곧 돌아오겠습니다.

kot tora-o-gesseumnida.

I have some baggage.

제가 짐이 있습니다.

chega jim-i isseumnida.

Where is the nearest bus stop?

가장 가까운 버스정거장이 어디 있습니까?

kajang kakkaun beoseu jeonggeojang-i eodi isseumnikka?

Is there a subway map in English?

영어로 된 지하철지도가 있습니까?

yeong-eoro doin jihach'eol jido-ga isseumnikka?

Which line goes to _____?

어느 노선이 _____에 갑니까?

eo-neu noseon-i _____ e kamnikka?

Does this bus go to _____?

이 버스가 _____에 갑니까?

i beoseuga_____e gamnikka?

City Hall	Euljiro
시청	을지로
sich'eong	euljjiro

Chongro	Sejongro
종로	세종로
chongno	sejongno

Where should I get off for _____?

_____에 가려면 어디서 내립니까?

_____e garyeo-myeon eodi-seo nae-rimnikka?

How many stops to_____?

_____은/는 몇번째 정거장입니까?

_____eun/neun   myeoppeon-jjae   jeonggeojang-imnikka?

I want to get off here.

여기서 내리고 싶습니다.

yeogiseo naerigo shipseumnida.

Please tell me when we get to _____.

_____에 도착하면 저에게 말씀해 주십시오.

_____ e doch'akhamyeon jeo-ege malsseumhae jushipshio.

How often do the buses run?

버스는 얼마나 자주 다닙니까?

peoseu-neun eolmana jaju danimnikka?

3. At the Hotel

Staying at a hotel in Korea will give you many chances to use the Korean language. The hotel staff will be glad to help, although many of them will be equally interested in practicing their English on you. Why not trade some of your English for Korean? In general, hotels in Korea that serve foreigners are equipped with many practical facilities. Most are spacious enough and comfortable, containing the usual basic furniture, accessories and amenities. Most hotels have Western rooms, but some hotels have both Western and traditional Korean rooms with ondol floors heated by a system of radiant pipes.

Hotels are classified into four types according to size, facilities and quality of service. They use roses of Sharon, the national flower of Korea, as a symbol of quality. Five flowers indicate deluxe class, four first class, three second class, and two third class. Major international credit cards are accepted by most hotels. Besides hotels there are traditional Korean style inns called yeogwan with ondol floors. Accomodations and services are traditional, providing a more homelike atmosphere. You may easily find a comfortable yeogwan in cities and in the countryside alike. Although prices are relatively low compared to hotels, the yeogwan may appeal to those who wish to experience more of the local culture.

(1) Staying at a hotel

I have a reservation.

저는 예약을 했습니다.

cheo-neun yeyak-eul haesseumnida.

I need a room for one night.

저는 하룻밤 묵을 방이 필요합니다.

cheo-neun harubam mukeul bang-i pillyohamnida.

I want a double room with a bath.

저는 목욕탕이 있는 큰 방을 원합니다.

cheo-neun mogyokt'ang-i inneun k'eun bang-eul
weonhamnida.

What is the rate for the room?

그 방값은 얼마입니까?

keu bangkapseun eolma-imnikka?

Where is the elevator?

엘리베이터가 어디에 있습니가?

elibeit'eo-ga eodi-e isseumnikka?

Please wake me tomorrow at 7 o'clock.

내일 일곱시에 깨워주십시오.

nae-il ilgopshi-e kkaeweo-jushipshiyo.

Did anyone call for me?

저한테 전화 온 것 있습니까?

cheo-hant'e jeonhwa on geo-isseumnikka?

I'd like to put this in the hotel safe.

이것을 호텔보관함에 두고 싶습니다.

igeoseul hot'el bogwanham-e dugo shipseumnida.

Can you please make this call for me?

이 전화 좀 걸어 주시겠습니까?

i jeonhwa jom georeo jushigesseumnikka?

Please send someone up for the bags.

짐꾼 좀 올려 보내주십시오.

chimkkun jom olyeo bonae-jushibshiyo.

I'd like the bill, please.

계산서 좀 주십시오.

kyesanseo jom chushipshiyo.

Major Hotels in Seoul
Ambassador
  186-54, 2-ga, Changch'ung-dong, Chung-gu

Hyatt Regency
   747-7, Hannam-dong, Youngsan-gu
King Sejong
   61-3, 2-ga, Ch'ungmu-ro, Chung-gu
Koreana
   61, 1-ga, Taep'yeong-ro, Chung-gu
Lotte
   1, Songong-dong, Chung-gu
President
   188-3, 1-ga, Eulchiro, Chung-gu
Riverside
   342-1 Shinsa-dong, Kangnam-gu
Hilton
   395, 5-ga, Namdaemun-ro
Palace
   528, Panp'o-dong, Kangnam-gu
Plaza
   23-1-ga, Taep'yeong-ro
Royal
   6-1-ga, Myeong-dong, Chung-gu
Sheraton Walker Hill
   San 21, Kwangjang-dong, Seongdong-gu
Shilla
   202, 2-ga, Changch'ung-dong, Chung-gu

(2) Making your flight reservation

When is there a flight to _____?

_____행 비행기는 언제 있습니까?

_____haeng bihaeng-gi-neun eonje isseumnikka?

Where do I pick up my luggage?

제 짐을 어디서 찾습니까?

che jim-eul eodiseo ch'at-sseumnikka?

That flight has been delayed/cancelled.

그 비행기가 연착/취소됐습니다.

keu bihaeng-gi-ga yeonch'ak/ch'ueso-dwaesseumnida.

May I carry this bag in the plane?

이 가방을 비행기에 가지고 타도 괜찮습니까?

i gabang-eul bihaeng-gi-e gajigo t'ado gwaench'
an-sseumnikka?

Your bags are overweight.

선생님의 가방무게가 초과되었습니다.

seonsaengnim-eui   gabangmuge-ga   ch'ogwa-
doeeosseumnida.

I'd like a seat in the_____.

나는 _____에 앉고 싶습니다.

na-neun_____e ankko sipsseumnida.

nonsmoking section	smoking section.
금연석	흡연석
keumyeon-seog	heubyeon-seog

near the window	on the aisle.
창가	통로옆
ch'ang-ga	t'ongro-yeop

What time does the plane leave?

몇시에 비행기가 떠납니까?

myeossi-e pihaenggi-ga tteonamnikka?

What's my flight number?

제 비행기(번호)는 몇번입니까?

che bihaeng-gi(beonho)-neun myeoppeon-imnikka?

What's the gate number?

출구(번호)는 몇번입니까?

ch'ulgu(beonho)-neun myeoppeon imnikka?

I'd like to confirm my flight reservation
제 비행기 예약을 확인하고 싶습니다.
che bihaenggi yeyak-eul hwag-in-hago shipseumnida.

(3) Renting a car

I would like to rent_____.
저는 _____를 빌리고 싶습니다.
cheoneun_____reul biligo shipsseumnida.
a car with automatic transmission
자동식 차 (chadongsik ch'a)
a small car
작은 차 (or 소형차)
chag-eun ch'a (or sohyeongch'a)
medium size car
중형차 (chunghyeongch'a)

How much does it cost per_____.
_____에 얼마입니까?
_____e eolma-imnikka?

day 하루(haru)   week 일주일(iljjuil)
kilometer 킬로당(k'irodang)

How much is the insurance?

보험료는 얼마입니까?

poheomryo-neun eolma-imnikka?

Do you accept credit cards?

신용카드를 받습니까?

shinyongk'adeu-reul basseumnikka?

Do I have to leave a deposit?

공탁금을 내야 합니까?

kongt'akgeum-eul nae-ya hamnikka?

I want to rent the car here.

여기서 차를 빌리고 싶습니다.

yeogiseo ch'a-reul biligo shipseumnida.

I would like to leave it in some place else.

다른 곳에 두고 싶습니다.

dareun gose dugo shipseumnida.

Where is the gas station?

주유소가 어디에 있습니까?

chuyuso-ga eodi-e isseumnikka?

Fill her up with premium

고급으로 가득 넣어주십시오.

kogeub-euro kadeuk neo-eo-jushipshiyo.

Please check the _____ .
_____ 을/를 좀 봐 주십시오.
_____ eul/reul jom bwajushipshiyo.

battery.   hood
바테리 bat'eri   보네트 ponet'eu

carburetor   oil
캬브레터   오일 oil
k'yabeuret'eo

                                  tires
spark plugs   타이어 t'aiyeo
스파크 플러그
seup'ak'eu p'euleogeu   water
                                  물 mul

(4) Leisure Time Activities

Wher can I buy _____ .
어디서 _____ 을/를 살 수 있습니까?
eodiseo _____ eul/reul salsu isseumnikka?

an English newspaper

영자신문 yeongjja shimmun

ticket	staff
표 pyo	지팡이 chip'ang-i

cap	rope
모자 moja	로프 rop'eu

dust bin
쓰레기통 sseuregit'ong

I'd like to see _____.
_____을/를 보고싶습니다.
_____eul bogo shipsseumnida.

a baseball game.	folk village
야구시합	민속촌
yagushihab	minsokch'on

Panmunjeom	Secret Garden
판문점	비원
panmunjeom	piweon

Where can I buy the tickets?
표를 어디서 살 수 있습니까?

p'yo-reul eodiseo sal su isseumnikka?

Is there a pool near the hotel?
호텔근처에 수영장이 있습니까?
hot'elgeunch'eo-e suyeongjang-i isseumnikka?

Is it far from here?
멉니까?
meomnikka?

Is there a dischotheque here?
이 근처에 디스코클럽이 있습니까?
igeunch'eo-e diseuk'o k'euleob-i isseumnikka?

Is there one at the hotel?
이 호텔에 있습니까?
ihot'el-e isseumnikka?

I would like to reserve a table.
자리를 예약하고 싶습니다.
chari-reul yeyakhago shipseumnida.

(5) Medical Care

Where is the nearest pharmacy?

가까운 약국이 어디 있습니까?

kakkaun yakkug-i eodi-e isseumnikka?

Is there a pharmacy that carries American medicine?

미제약을 파는 약국이 있습니까?

mijeyag-eul p'a-neun yakkug-i isseumnikka?

I need something for ____.

나는 ____ 약이 필요합니다.

na-neun kamgiyag-i p'ilyohamnida.

a cold	indigestion
감기 kamgi	소화불량 sohwa bullyang
constipation	insomnia
변비 pyeonbi	불면증 pulmyeonjjeung
a cough	a toothache
기침 kich'im	치통 ch'it'ong
diarrhea	an upset stomach
설사 seolsa	위통 wit'ong

a headache 두통 tut'ong

I don't feel well.
몸이 좀 불편합니다.
mom-i jom bulp'yeon-hamnida.

I need a doctor who speaks English.
영어를 할 수 있는 의사가 필요합니다.
yeong-eoreul halsu inneun euisaga p'iryohamnida.

I'm dizzy.
어지럽습니다.
eojireopsseumnida.

I feel weak.
기운이 없습니다.
giun-i eopsseumnida.

I have a pain in my chest around my heart.
심장부근 가슴이 아픕니다.
shimjangbugeun gaseum-i ap'eumnida.

I had a heart attack some years ago.
몇년전 심장마비에 걸렸었습니다.

myeonnyeonjeon shimjangmabi-e geolyeosseousseumnida.

I'm taking this medicine.
이 약을 쓰고 있습니다.
iyag-eul sseugo isseumnida.

Do I have to go to the hospital?
병원에 가야 합니까?
pyeong-weone gaya hamnikka?

I have a toothache.
치통이 있습니다.
ch'itong-i isseumnida.

Could you recommend a dentist?
치과의사를 소개해 주시겠습니까?
ch'ikkwa-euisa-reul sogae-hae jushigesseumnikka?

I just broke my glasses.
제 안경이 방금 깨졌습니다.
che angyeong-i bang-geum kkaejyeosseumnida.

Can you repair them while I wait?
기다리는 동안 고쳐 주실 수 있습니까?

kidarineun dong-an goch'yeo jushil su isseumnikka?

(3) Telephone Conversation

You are wanted on the phone.

전화왔어요.

cheonhwa-oasseoyo.

Hello. who is this?

여보세요. 누구세요?

yeoboseyo. nugu-seyo.

This is _____.

저는 _____입니다.

cheoneun _____ imnida.

May I speak with _____?

_____와 통화할 수 있습니까?

_____ oa t'onghwa-hal su isseumnikka?

Hello. I want 555-1111 please.

여보세요. 오오오의 일일일번 좀 부탁합니다.

yeoboseyo. o-o-o-e il-il-il-beon jom but'akhamnida.

Hello. Please connect me with the Lottel Hotel.

여보세요, 롯데호텔 좀 연결해주세요.
yeoboseyo, lotte hot'el jom yeon-gyeol-hae juseyo.

I'm sorry, the line is busy.
죄송합니다만 통화중입니다.
choisonghamnida-man t'onghwajung-imnida.

No one answers.
전화받지 않습니다.
cheonhwa-bajji ansseumnida.

Thanks. I'll try again later.
감사합니다. 나중에 걸겠습니다.
kamsahamnida. najung-e geolgesseumnida.

Please give him a message.
내용 좀 전해주세요.
naeyong jom jeonhaejuseyo.

Operator, I dialed the wrong number.
교환 아가씨 번호를 잘못 돌렸습니다.
kyohwan agassi beonhoreul jalmot-tolryeosseumnida.

I can't speak Korean.

저는 한국어를 못합니다.

cheo-neun hankuk-eo reul mot-hamnida.

Please speak English.

영어로 좀 말해주세요.

yeong-eoro jom malhae-juseyo.

Were there any calls for me?

저에게 전화 온 것이 있습니까?

cheo-ege jeonhwa on geoshi isseumnikka?

Yes. Mr. Kim called.

네, 김씨가 전화했습니다.

ne kimssi-ga jeonhwa haesseumnida.

Here's his telephone number.

여기 그의 전화번호가 있습니다.

yeogi geu-eui jeonhwa-beonho-ga isseumnida.

The telephone is our of order.

전화기가 고장났습니다.

jeonhwagi-ga gojangnasseumnida.

May I have a telephone directory?

전화번호부좀 볼까요?

cheonhwa-beonhobu jom bolkkayo?

I want to call my home.

집에 전화하고 싶습니다.

chib-e jeonhwahago shipsseumnida.

What time is it in the United States now?

미국에서는 지금 몇시죠?

migug-eseo-neun jigeum myeosshijyo?

Where is a public telephone?

공중전화가 어디에 있습니까?

kongjungjeonhwa-ga eodi-e isseumnikka?

Is there an English telephone directory?

영어로 된 전화번호부가 있습니까?

yeong-eo-ro doin jeonhwabeonhobu-ga isseumnikka?

I'd like to make a phone call.

전화를 걸려고 합니다.

cheonhwa-reul geolyeogo hamnida.

Could you give me some change?

잔돈좀 주시겠습니까?
chandon jom jushigesseumnikka?

May I use your phone?
댁의 전화좀 써도 괜찮습니까?
taeg-eui jeonhwa jom sseodo gwench'anseumnikka?

How do you call the United States?
미국에 어떻게 전화합니까?
migug-e eotteok'e jeonhwa-hamnikka?

How do you call Canada?
카나다에 어떻게 전화합니까?
k'anada-e eotteok'e jeonhwa-hamnikka?

How do you call Australia?
호주에 어떻게 전화합니까?
hoju-e eotteok'e jeonhwa-hamnikka?

How do you call England?
영국에 어떻게 전화합니까?
yeonggug-e eotteok'e jeonhwa-hamnikka?

I'd like to talk to the operator.

교환양과 전화하고 싶습니다.
kyohwan-yang-gwa jeonhwa-hago shipseumnida.

May I speak to_____?
_____ 좀 바구어 주시겠습니까?
_____ jom bakkweo jushigesseumnikka?

Who's calling?
누구십니까?
nugushimnikka?

Speak slowly, please.
천천히 말씀해 주십시오.
ch'eonch'eon-hi malsseumhae jushipshio.

Speak louder please.
크게 말씀해주십시오.
k'euge malsseum-hae jushipshio.

Don't hang up.
끊지 마십시오.
kkeunch'i mashipshiyo.

I got a wrong munber.

잘못 걸었습니다.
chalmot keor-eosseumnida.

I was disconnected.
연결이 안됐습니다.
yeongyeor-i andwaesseumnida.

I would like to leave a message.
말씀 좀 전해주시겠습니까?
malsseum jom jeonhae jushigesseumnikka?

He/She isn't here.
그분이 여기 안계십니다.
keubun-i yeo-gi an-gyeshimnida.

The line is busy.
통화중입니다.
t'onghwajung-imnida.

He/She'll be back at _____ .
그분은 _____ 에 돌아오십니다.
keubun- eun _____ e dora-oshimnida.

He's _____ .

그분은 _____ 입니다.
keubun-eun _____ imnida.

in a meeting.	out to lunch
회의중 hoeeuijung	점심식사중 jeomshimshiksajung

on vacation
휴가중 hyugajung

(7) Postal Service

mailbox	telegram
우체통 uch'etong	전보 cheonbo
post office	air-mail letter
우체국 uch'eguk	항공편지 hang-gong p'yeonji
post card	registered letter
엽서 yeopseo	등기편지 teung-gi p'yeonji
letter	special delivery letter
편지 p'yeonji	속달편지 sokttal p'yeonji

Where is a mailbox?
우체통이 어디에 있습니까?

uch'etong-i eodi-e isseumnikka?

I'd like to buy some stamps.
나는 우표를 사려고 합니다.
naneun up'yo-reul saryeogo hamnida.

Which window is it?
어느 창구입니까?
eo-neu ch'ang-guimnikka?

What's the postage to the United States?
미국까지 우편요금은 얼마입니까?
mi-guk-kkaji upyeonyogeum-eun eolmaimnikka?

I'd like to send a telex.
텔렉스로 보내려고 합니다.
t'elex-ro bonaeryeogo hamnida.

How late are you open?
몇시까지 엽니까?
myeosshi-kkaji yeomnikka?

How much is it per_____?
_____에 얼마입니까?

_____ e eolma-imnikka?

minute?   word
일분에(ilbun-e)   한단어에(han-dan-eo-e)

4. Dining

Koreans are not accustomed to eating while driving or walking along the street. However making food is one of the glories of Korean culture and one you can delight daily. Breakfast, lunch, and dinner times in Korea are similar to customs almost everywhere else. Visitors to Korea often eat at assigned tables from a specially prepared hotel menu. If you have special dietary needs or are allergic to certain kinds of food, make your requests in advance for help. Make a list of the foods that don't agree with you and try to learn to say them in Korea. Here is a handy guide.

I can't eat _____.　　저는 _____을 먹지 못합니다. 　cheoneun _____ eul meokchi mot'amnida.

Often at the table you will be given chopsticks. Don't worry though, because knives and forks also are always available.

Restaurants abound in Korea. One is never far away. Eating establishments vary from fast food ramyeon and coffee shops to buffet in large cities. There are many menus to choose from. Some different regions specialize in their own traditional foods. For example, hanjeongsik or pibimbab is well known for its various kinds.

Don't expect to be able to make a reservation at every

restaurant. Generally, only first-rate restaurants will accept reservations. Be prepared to wait more than 20 minutes for a table at a popular restaurant.

Alcholic beverages are not so expensive as in western countries. Tipping is not customary in restaurants. Bars and discoteques serve alcohol but no regular food. However, they stay open until midnight.

(1) At a Hotel Restaurant

Is there a restaurant in the hotel?

호텔에 식당이 있습니까?

hot'el-e shikttang-i isseumnikka?

Yes, there is.

예 있습니다.

ye isseumnida.

What floor is it on?

몇층에 있습니까?

myeoch'eung-e isseumnikka?

It's on the third floor.

3층에 있습니다.

samch'eung-e isseumnida.

What time do we eat dinner?

몇시에 저녁을 먹습니까?

myeosshi-e jeo-nyeogeul meoksseumnikka?

We eat dinner at six.
여섯시에 저녁을 먹습니다.
yeoseoshi-e jeonyeog-eul meoksseumnida.

Are you hungry?
배고프십니까?
paegop'eushimnikka?

Very hungry.
매우 배고픕니다.
maeu paegop'eumnida.

(2) Eating out

Where are we going to eat?
어디에서 먹나요?
eodieseo meongnayo?

Let's eat out tonight.
오늘저녁 외식합시다.
oneul jeo-nyeog oisikhapshida.

Where is a good restaurant?
유명한 식당이 어디에 있습니까?
yumyeonghan shikttang-i eodi-e isseumnikka?

What's it called?
이름이 무엇입니까?
ireum-i mueoshimnikka?

It's called _____.
이름은 _____입니다.
ireum-eun _____ imnida.

Is it far from here?
여기서 먼가요?
yeogiseo meongayo?

No, it's very close.
아니요, 매우 가까이 있습니다.
aniyo, maeu gakkai isseumnida.

What sort of food do they serve?
어떤 음식이 나오나요?
eotteon eumshig-i naonayo?

They serve various kinds of food.
여러종류의 음식이 있습니다.
yeoreo jongryu-eui eumshig-i isseumnida.

Please call a taxi for us.
택시좀 불러주세요.
t'aekssi jom buleojuseyo.

Can you help me find a restaurant?
음식점 좀 찾아 주세요.
eumshikjjeom jom ch'aja juseyo.

I want to reserve a table.
테이블을 예약하고 싶습니다.
t'eibeul-eul yeyakhago shipsseumnida.

What time are you coming?
몇시에 오시겠습니까?
myeoshi-e oshigesseumnikka?

We'll arrive at six.
6시에 오겠습니다.
yeoseossi-e ogesseumnida.

How many altogether?
모두 몇명입니까?
modu myeonmyeong-imnikka?

Altogether there will be eight people.
모두 열명입니다.
modu yeolmyeong-imnida.

How much per person?
1인당 얼마입니가?
irindang eolma-imnikka?

5000 won per person for _____ .

_____먹는 데 1인당 오천원입니다.

_____meongneunde irindang och'eon-weon-imnida.

breakfast
아침식사
ach'im-shiksa

lunch
점심식사
cheom-shimshiksa

dinner
저녁식사
cheonyeog-shiksa

Korean food
한식
han-shik

Chinese food
중국음식
chung-gug eumshik

Japanese food
화식
hwashik

Western food
양식
yangshik

Korean restaurant
한식집
hanshigkjjib

Chinese restaurant
중국집
chunggukjjib

Japanese restaurant
일식집
ilshikjjib

Western restaurant
양식집
yangshikjjib

Do you know a good restaurant?
좋은 음식점을 아십니까?
cho-eun eumshikcheom-eul ashimnikka?

Is it very expensive?
매우 비쌉니까?
maeu pissamnikka?

Waiter!/Waitress!
웨이터/웨이트레스
weit'eo/weit'res

We'd like to have lunch.
점심먹고 싶습니다.
cheomshimmeoggo shipseumnida.

I'd like to try Korean food.
한식을 먹어보고 싶습니다.
hanshigeul meogeobogo shipseumnida.

The menu, please.
메뉴 좀 주십시오.
menyu jom jushipshio.

What's today's special?
오늘 특식은 무엇입니까?
oneul t'eukshik-eun mueoshimnikka?

What do you recommend?
무슨 음식을 권하시겠습니까?
museun eumshig-eul gweonhasshigesseumnikka?

To begin with, please bring us a cocktail.
먼저 칵테일 좀 가져다 주십시오.
meonjeo k'akt'eil jom gajeoda jushipshio.

a bottle of mineral water
약수한병
yaksu hanbyeong

a beer
맥주한병
maekchu hanbyeong

Do you have grape wine?
포도주 있습니까?
p'odoju isseumnikka?

I'd like to order now.
지금 주문하고 싶습니다.
chigeum jumunhago shipseumnida.

Show me the menu again, please.
메뉴 좀 다시 보여주십시오.
menyu jom dashi boyeo jushibsio.

I'd like some coffee, please.
커피좀 주십시오.
k'eop'i jom jushibshio.

Do you have American cigarettes?

미국담배 있습니까?

miguk dambae isseumnikka?

Please give me a pack of matches also.

성냥도 좀 주십시오.

seongnyangdo jom jushipshio.

Do you mind if I smoke?

담배피워도 괜찮습니까?

tampae p'iweodo gwanch'ansseumnikka?

Check, please.

계산서좀 주십시오.

kyesanseo jom jushipshio.

Do you take _____?

_____을/를 받습니까?

_____eul/reul basseumnikka?

credit cards	traveller's checks
신용카드	여행자 수표
shinyong k'adeu	yeohaengja sup'yo

Which credit cards do you take?

어떤 신용카드를 받습니까?

eotteon shinyong k'adeu-reul basseumnikka?

Are the tax and service charge included?

세금과 서비스가 포함됐습니까?

segeumgwa seobiseu-ga p'ohamdwaesseumnikka?

Is this correct?

이것이 맞습니까?

igeoshi masseumnikka?

May I have a receipt, please?

영수증 좀 주시겠어요?

yeongsujeung jom jushigesseoyo?

We don't have much time.

우리는 시간이 없습니다.

urineun shigan-i eopsseumnida.

Where are the restrooms?

화장실이 어디에 있습니까?

hwajangshiri eodi-e isseumnikka?

Could you bring me _____ please?

_____좀 가져다 주시겠습니가?

_____jom gajyeoda jushigesseumnikka?

a knife   a spoon
칼(k'al)   숟가락(sukkarak)

a table spoon
차 숟가락
ch'a sukkarak

a saucer
잔 받침대
chan batch'imdae

a glass
잔(chan)

a plate
접시(cheopshi)

a cup
컵(k'eop)

a bowl
그릇(keureut)

a napkin
내프킨(naep'euk'in)

a toothpick
이쑤시게(issushigae)

an ashtray
재털이(chaet'eori)

(3) To the waiter

I want to eat with chopsticks.
젓가락을 가지고 먹고 싶습니다.
cheokkarak-eul gajigo meokko shipsseumnida.

Please show me how to hold the chopsticks.
젓가락 집는 방법좀 알려 주십시오.
cheokkark jimneun bangbeob jom alyeojushipshyo.

I can't use chopsticks.

저는 저붐을 사용할 수 없습니다.
cheoneun jeobumeul sayonghal su eopsseumnida.

Please give me a knife and fork
나이프와 포크 좀 주십시오.
naip'eu-oa p'ok'eu jom jushipshyo.

(4) Different Dishes

pork
돼지고기 (twaejigogi)

soup
수프 (sup'eu)

beef
소고기 (sogogi)

chicken
닭고기 (takkogi)

fish
생선 (saengseon)

shrimp
새우 (saeu)

vegetable
채소 (ch'aeso)

noodles
국수 (kuk-su)

Please bring me _____.
_____ 좀 주십시오.
_____jom jushipshyo.

a glass of water
물한잔 (mul hanjan)

a bottle of wine
술한병 (sul hanbyeong)

a pair of chopsticks
젓가락 한쌍
cheokkarak hanssang

a fork
포크 하나(p'okeu hana)

a spoon
스푼(seup'un hana)

a glass
유리잔하나
yurijan hana

a napkin
내프킨(naep'euk'in)

a bowl
주발(chubal)

some pepper
후추(huch'u)

two cups of coffee
커피 두잔(k'eop'i dujan)

a knife
나이프 하나
naipeu hana

a dish
그릇하나(keureut hana)

two bottles of beer
맥주 두병
maekchu dubyeong

bread
빵(ppang)

an ashtray
재털이(chaet'eol-i)

some sugar
설탕(seolt'ang)

some hot pepper
좀 매운 후추
jom maeun huch'u

(5) If there is a problem

I can't eat, please take it away.

먹을 수 없으니 치워주세요.

meogeul su eopsseuni ch'iweo juseyo.

We have ordered the wrong food.

음식을 잘못 시켰습니다.

eumshik-eul jalmot shik'yeosseumnida.

We would like to order some more food.

음식을 좀 더 시키고 싶습니다.

eumshigeul jom deo shik'igo shipsseumnida.

I don't like this.

저는 이것을 좋아하지 않습니다.

cheoneun igeosseul joahaji annsseumnida.

I'm allergic to _____.

저는 _____에 알레르기가 있습니다.

cheoneun _____ e alereugiga isseumnida.

Does this dish contain _____?

이 음식에 _____이 들었습니까?

i eumshig-e _____ i deuleosseumnikka?

There is a mistake on the bill.

계산서가 잘못되어 있는 것 같습니다.

kyesanseo-ga jalmoddeoi-eo-inneun geo gasseumnida.

Please check it over.

다시 한번 확인해 주십시오.

tashi hanbeon hoag-in hae jushipshio.

May I speak to the manager?

지배인에게 말씀해 드릴까요?

chibae-in-ege malsseum-hae deurilkkayo?

Do you accept personal checks?

자기앞 수표도 받습니까?

chagi-ap supyodo basseumnikka.

May I pay with a traveller's check?

여행자 수표로 지불해도 되나요?

yeohaengja supyoro jibulhaedodoinayo?

Where do we pay?

어디서 지불하나요?

eodiseo jibulhanayo.

I'm full.

저는 배가 부른데요.

cheoneun baega bureundeyo.

I've had enough.
많이 먹었습니다.
man-i meogeosseumnida.

(6) Common Foods

1) Meats

beef
쇠고기(soigogi)

lamb
양고기(yang-gogi)

chicken
닭고기(takkogi)

ham
햄(haem)

duck
오리고기(origogi)

pork
돼지고기(toejigogi)

steak
스테이크(seuteik'eu)

sausage
소시지(soshiji)

spare ribs
갈비(kalbi)

hamburger
햄버거(hamburger)

cooked rare(underdone)
설익은
(seol-igeun)

roasted
로스한(roseu-han)

fried
후라이한(hurai-khan)

cooked medium
반쯤 익은
panjjeum igeun

cooked well-done
잘익은
chal igeun

tough
질긴(chilgin)

tender
연한(yeonhan)

2) Vegetables

rice(plain, boiled)
밥(pab)

fried rice
비빔밥(pibimbab)

potatoes
감자(kamja)

sweet potatoes
고구마(koguma)

beans
콩(k'ong)

mushrooms
버섯(peoseot)

onions
양파(yangp'a)

cucumber
오이(o-i)

tomatoes
토마도(tomado)

garlic
마늘(maneul)

3) Fruits

orange
오렌지(orenji)

lemon
레몬(remon)

apple
사과(sagwa)

each
복숭아(pokssung-a)

pear
배(pae)

melon
멜론(melon)

banana
바나나(banana)

4) Desserts

ice cream
아이스 크림(aiseu k'eurim)

fruit
과일(kwa-il)

cookies
과자(kwaja)

crackers
크랙카
(k'euraek'a)

candy
캔디
(k'aendi)

pudding
푸딩
(pu'ding)

cake
케익
(k'eikeu)

sweets
사탕(sat'ang)

5) Drinks

(boiled) water
(끓인)물(mul)

brandy
브랜디(peuraendi)

tea
차(ch'a)

whisky
위스키(wisk'i)

coffee
커피(k'eop'i)

beer
맥주(maekchu)

lemonade
레몬쥬스(remon jyuseu)

orange juice
오렌지쥬스(orenji jyuseu)

milk
우유(uyu)

green tea
녹차(nokch'a)

black tea
흑차(heukch'a)

6) Miscellaneous

soy sauce
간장(kanjang)

cheese
치즈(ch'ijeu)

sugar
설탕(seolt'ang)

butter
버터(peot'eo)

mustard
겨자(kyeoja)

hungry
목마른(mongmareun)

bill
청구서(ch'eong-gu-seo)

men's room
남자화장실

(namjahwajangshil)

menu
메뉴(menyu)

chopsticks
젖가락(cheokkarak)

waiter/waitress
웨이터/웨이트리스
(weiteo/weiteuriseu)

tea spoon
차숫갈(ch'asukkal)

soup spoon
국자(kugjja)

knife
칼(k'al)

a glass of
한잔의
(hanjaneui)

fork
포크(p'okeu)

spoon
스푼(seup'eun)

a bottle of _____
한병의_____
(hanbyeong-eui)

food sotre
식료품점
shingnyop'umjeom

snack shop
간이식당
kan-ishikttang

snacks
스낵(seunaek)

restaurant
식당(shikttang)

breakfast
아침(ach'im)

dining hall
연회실(yeonhoeshil)

lunch
점심(cheomshim)

tasty
맛있는(massinneun)

dinner
저녁(cheonyeok)

salt
소금(sogeum)

pepper
후추(huch'u)

vinegar
식초(shikch'o)

oil
기름(kireum)

7) Tastes

hot(peppery)
매운(maeun)

salty
짠(jjan)

sweet
단(tan)

bitter
쓴(sseun)

sour
신(shin)

5. Shopping

In the capital of Seoul, one of the most popular places for foreigners to shop is It'aeweon near the U. S. Army base in Yongsan. Insadong and Myeongdong are also popular. There the prices are somewhat higher than at other local markets, but you can haggle or bargain over prices. Most downtown stores are open from 10.00 A.M. and remain open as late as midnight almost every day.

Besides department stores, there are various kinds of shopping places such as arcades, specialized shopping districts, open air markets, and duty-free shops for foreign tourists and shoppers.

(1) Useful Expressions

I want to go shopping.
쇼핑하고 싶습니다.
syop'inghago shipseumnida.

What do you want to buy?
무엇을 사려고 하십니까?
mueosseul saryeogo hashimnikka?

I want to buy_____.
저는 _____을 사고 싶습니다.
cheo-neun _____ eul sago shipseumnida.

a painting
그림(keurim)

a piece of pottery
도자기(tojagi)

an antique
골동품(koldongp'eum)

a silk scarf
실크스카프(shilkeusk'apeu)

rice wine
쌀막걸리(ssal makkeoli)

a book
책(ch'aek)

a woolen swater
털스웨터(t'eolseu-wet'eo)

a hat
모자(moja)

an overcoat
외투(oet'u)

a rug
양탄자(yangt'anja)

a piece of jewelry
보석류(poseokryu)

a silk tie
실크타이(shilkeut'ai)

a pair of shoes
구두(kudu)

a pair of socks
양말(yangmal)

perfume
향수(hyangsu)

a blause
블라우스(pulauseu)

underwear
속내의(songnae-ue)

What time do the stores open?

몇시에 상점이 문을 엽니까?

myeossi-e sangjeom-i mun-eul yeomnikka?

The stores open at nine.

저 상점은 9시에 문을 엽니다.

cheo sangjeom-eun ahopshi-e mun-eul yeomnida.

What time do the stores close?

몇시에 상점이 문을 닫습니까?

myeossi-e sangjeom-i mun-eul dasseumnik-ka?

They close at seven.

상점들이 7시에 문을 닫습니다.

sangjeomdeul-i ilgopshi-e mun-eul dasseumnida.

Where do foreigners shop?

외국인들은 어디서 쇼핑합니까?

oigug-indeul-eun eodiseo syop'ing-eul hamnikka?

Foreigners can shop at It'aeweon.

외국인들은 이태원에서 쇼핑할 수 있습니다.

oigug-indeul-eun it'aeweon-eseo syop'inghal su isseumnida.

Insadong	Myeongdong
인사동(insadong)	명동(myeongdong)

Is it far?
거리가 먼가요?
keoriga meongayo?

No, it's nearby.
아니요, 가까이에 있습니다.
aniyo, kakkai-e isseumnida.

How can I get there?
어떻게 갈 수 있습니까?
eotteoge galsu isseumnikka?

You can walk or go by taxi.
걸어서 가거나 택시로 갈 수 있습니다.
keoreoseo gageona t'aekshiro gal su isseumnida.

You can take a bus.
버스타고 갈 수 있습니다.
peoseu-t'ago kal su isseumnida.

How much is it?
그것은 얼마입니까?
keugeosseun eolmaimnikka?

Where can I find _____?
_____을/를 어디서 찾을 수 있습니까?
_____ eul/reul eodiseo ch'ajeul su isseumnikka?

Can you help me?

좀 도와주실 수 있습니까?

chom dowa jushil su isseumnikka?

I need _____.

_____이/가 필요합니다.

_____i/ga p'iryohamnida.

Do you have any others?

다른 것이 있습니까?

tareun geoshi isseumnikka?

Do you have anything _____?

_____인/한 것이 있습니까?

_____in/han geoshi isseumnikka?

smaller?	yellow?
더 작은(deo jageun)	노란색의(noransaeg-eui)
larger?	red?
더 큰(deo k'keun)	붉은색의(burgeunsaeg-eui)

Can I pay with a traveler's check?

여행자 수표를 드려도 됩니까?

yeohaengja sup'yo-reul deuryeodo doemnikka?

(2) Shops and Stores

I would like to go to _____.
_____에 가고 싶습니다.
_____ e gago shipsseumnida.

store
가게(kage)

barber shop
이발소(ibalso)

market
시장(shijang)

beauty parlor
미장원(mijangweon)

department store
백화점(paek-hwajeom)

stationery
문방구(munbang-gu)

bakery
제과점(chegwajeom)

souvenir store
기념품가게
(kinyemp'um-gage)

shoe store
양화점(yanghwajeom)

book store
책방(ch'aekppang)

tailor shop
양복점(yangbokcheom)

gas station
주유소(chuyuso)

dressmaking store
양장점(yangjangjeom)

florist
꽃가게(kkokkage)

antique store
골동품점
(kolttongp'umjeom)

tobacco store
담배가게(tambae gage)

general store
잡화점(chaphwajeom)

street stall
노점(nojeom)

laundry
세탁소(set'akso)

Do you want to drop in _____?
_____에 들리고 싶습니까?
_____ e deuligo shipsseumnikka?

How much is it?
그것은 얼마입니까?
keugeosseun eolmaimnikka?

Where can I find _____?
_____을/를 어디서 찾을 수 있습니까?
_____ eul/reul eodiseo ch'ajeul su isseumnikka?

Can you help me?
좀 도와주실 수 있습니까?
chom dowajushil su isseumnikka?

I need_____.

_____이 있습니까.
_____i isseumnikka.

Do you have any others?
다른 것이 있습니까?
tareun geoshi isseumnikka?

Do you have anything_____?
_____이/가 필요합니까?
_____i/ga p'iryohamnikk?

Hello. I am a foreigner.
여보세요 저는 외국사람입니다.
yeoboseyo cheo-neun oigug saramimnida.

Can you help me?
도와주시겠어요?
dowa jushigesseoyo?

Are you the salesperson?
당신은 판매원입니까?
tangshineun p'anmaeweonimnikka?

Welcome. what do you wish to buy?
어서 오세요. 무엇을 사려고 합니까?
eoseo oseyo. mueoseul saryeogo hamnikka?

Do you have any_____?

_____을 가지고 있습니까?

_____eul kajigo isseumnikka?

(3) About Prices

How much is this?

이것은 얼마입니까?

igeoseun eolmaimnikka?

That costs_____.

그것은 _____입니다.

keugeosseun_____imnida.

five hundred won
오백원(obaegweon)

two thousand won
이천원(ich'eonweon)

one hundred won
백원(baegweon)

That's too expensive.

그것은 너무 비쌉니다.

keugeosseun neomu bissamnida.

I don't like this color.

이 색깔은 마음에 들지 않습니다.

i saekkal-eun maum-e deulji anseumnida.

I do'nt like this style.

이 스타일은 마음에 들지 않습니다.

ist'ail-eun maeum-e deulji anseumnida.

This is the wrong size.

사이즈가 틀립니다.

saijeuga t'eulimnida.

I'd like to see another.

다른 것 좀 보고 싶습니다.

tareun keojjom bogo shipseumnida.

Please show me a _____.

_____ 좀 보여주십시오.

_____ jom poyeojushipshiyo.

larger size
보다 큰 사이즈
poda k'eun saijeu

cheaper one
보다 값이 싼 것
poda gapshi ssan keot

smaller size
보다 작은 사이즈
poda jageun saijeu

Please take my measurements.

재어주세요.

chae-eo juseyo.

What size shoes do you wear?

몇 사이즈 크기의 구두를 신나요?

myeossaijeu-eui gudu-reul shinnayo?

I wear size seven.

사이즈 7을 신습니다.

saijeu ch'ileul shinseumnida.

This is too small.

이것은 너무나 작습니다.

igeoseun neomuna chakseumnida.

This is too big.

이것은 너무나 큽니다.

igeoseun neomuna k'eumnida.

(4) Buying a Gift

I want to buy a gift for _____.

나는 _____에게 줄 선물을 사고 싶습니다.

naneun _____ege jul seonmul-eul sago shipseumnida.

my friend 나의 친구 na-eui ch'in-gu	my wife 나의 아내 na-eui ane
my husband 나의 남편	a child 아기

na-eui namp'yeon   agi

I want a _____ one.
나는 _____것을 원합니다.
na-neun _____geoseul weonhamnida.

blue 푸른(p'ureun)	yellow 노랑색의(norang saekeui)
black 검은(geomeun)	pink 핑크색의(p'ink saekeui)
brown 갈색의(galsaegeui)	gray 회색의(hoi saekeui)
green 초록의(ch'orogui)	bright coloered 밝은색의(balgeun saekeui)
white 흰색의(hin saegeui)	dark colored 짙은 색의(jit'eun saekeui)
red 붉은 색의(bulgeun saegeui)	bright red 선홍색의(seonhong saekeui)
larger 보다 큰(boda k'eun)	another(different one) 다른(dareun)

smaller
보다 작은(boda chag-eun)

> This is too _____.
> 이것은 너무나 _____ 입/합니다.
> igeosseun neomuna_____im/hamnida.

long
긴(gin)

wide
넓은(neorbeun)

short
짧은(jjarbeun)

narrow
좁은(jobeun)

small
작은(jag-eun)

tight
꼭 죄는(kkog joineun)

large
큰(k'eun)

bright
밝은(balgeun)

(5) What a shopkeeper might say

> Good morning sir.
> 안녕하세요?
> annyeong-haseyo?

> What do you want to buy?
> 무엇을 사려고 하십니까?
> mueosseul saryeogo hashimnikka?

How many?
얼마나요?
eolmanayo?

What size?
크기는요?
k'eugi-neun yo?

What color do you want?
무슨 색상을 원하십니까?
museun saeksang-eul weonhashimnikka?

Do you want to try it on?
입어보고 싶습니까?
ib-eo-bogo shipseumnikka?

Is this one all right?
이것이 맞는 것입니까?
igeoshi manneun geoshimnikka?

I will show you another.
다른 것을 보여 드리겠습니다.
tareun geoseul boyeo deurigesseumnida.

Do you want anything else?
이외에도 다른 것을 또 원하십니까?
i-oi-edo dareun geoseul tto weonhashimnikka?

Will you take it with you?

가져가시겠습니까?

kajyeogashigesseumnikka?

We will send it to your hotel.

호텔까지 보내 드리겠습니다.

hot'elkkaji bonae deurigesseumnida.

Shall we ship it to your home?

선편으로 보내 드릴까요?

seonp'yeon-euro bonae deurilkkayo?

Please write down your address.

주소 좀 적어주십시오.

chuso jom jeog-eo jushipshiyo.

We don't have any_____.

저희는 _____이 없습니다.

cheowhi-neun_____i eopsseumnida.

Here is your bill.

여기 청구서가 있습니다.

yeogi ch'eongguseo-ga isseumnida.

Here is your change.

여기 거스름돈이 있습니다.

yeogi geoseureumdon-i isseumnida.

This is your receipt.

여기 영수증이 있습니다.

yeogi yeongsujeung-i isseumnida.

Please come again.

또 오십시오.

tto oshipshi-yo.

6. Sightseeing

Sightseeing will naturally be one of your major activities in Korea and it will be a great reward to you. Where you go will depend on your particular personal interests. If you join a tour, choose one that visits the areas you want to see.

Local buses are overcrowded throughout downtown Seoul. However, they run very quickly and efficiently and are very convenient for traveling anywhere in the city. The bus fare is 210 won for a bus token.

Express buses running on major highways are very convenient and efficient in traveling between major cities.

(1) About the weather

What is the weather like?

날씨가 어떻습니까?

nalssiga eotteosseumnikka?

It is beautiful.

화창합니다.

hwach'anghamnida.

It is hot.

덥습니다.

teopseumnida.

It is very hot.
매우 덥습니다.
mae-u deopseumnida.

It is sunny.
맑습니다.
maksseumnida.

It is bad.
좋지 않습니다.
choch'i ansseumnida.

It is cool.
시원합니다.
shiweonhamnida.

It is cold.
춥습니다.
ch'upsseumnida.

It is very cold.
매우 춥습니다.
mae-u ch'upsseumnida.

It is windy.
바람이 붑니다.
parami bumnida.

It is foggy.
안개꼈었습니다.
angaekki-eosseumnida.

It is raining.
비옵니다.
piomnida.

Is it going to rain today?
오늘 비올까요?
o-neul biolkkayo?

It's too hot to go out.
외출하기에는 너무 덥습니다.
oech'ulhagi-e-neun neomu deopsseumnida.

(2) Visiting various places

Never fail to visit the museums. They are the places where the best things you have to see in the country are preserved. If you are on a tight schedule, don't spend too much of your time on window shopping, browsing around the stores, or on shopping. For those who remain home, a small, inexpensive souvenir, which is also light to carry, will do.

Mingle with the people of the country and get acquainted. Don't always stay in your own group. Have curiosity, and try to understand the people. Read the local newspapers, listen to the radio, and watch television and you will get much information.

I would like to go to see _____ .
나는 _____보러 가고 싶습니다.
naneun _____ boreo gago shipseumnida.

I would like to go sightseeing.
나는 관광하고 싶습니다.
na-neun kwan-gwanghago shipseumnida.

What are we going to see?
우리는 무엇을 보러갑니까?
uri-neun mueosseul boreo gamnikka?

We are going to see _____ .
우리는 _____보러 갑니다.
uri-neun _____ boreo gamnida.

How long will the tour last?
여행은 얼마나 계속합니까?
yeohaeng-eun eolmana gyesokhamnikka?

one hour   two hours
한시갇(hanshigan)   두시간(tushigan)

Are you our guide?

당신이 안내자입니까?
tangshin-i annaejaimnikka?

No, the man over there is our guide.
아니요, 저기있는 사람이 우리의 안내자입니다.
aniyo, jeogi-inneun saram-i urieui anaeja-imnida.

May I ask his name?
그분의 성함이 무엇입니까?
keubuneui seongham-i mueoshimnikka?

He is called Kim Myeong Su.
그의 성함은 김명수입니다.
keu-eui seongham-eun kimmyueongsu-imnida.

Do you speak English?
영어를 말하십니까?
yeong-eo reul malhashimnikka?

I only speak a few words of English.
나는 영어를 조금밖에 못합니다.
na-neun yeong-eo-reul jogeumbakke mot'amnida.

What time will the tour start?
몇시에 여행이 시작됩니까?
myeoshi-e yheohaeng-i shijagdoimnikka?

We'll leave the hotel at nine A.M.
아침 7시에 호텔을 출발합니다.
ach'im ilgopshi-e hotel-eul ch'ulbalhamnida.

What time will we return?
몇시에 돌아옵니까?
myeoshi-e doraomnikka?

We'll return at 3 P.M.
3시에 돌아옵니다.
seshie doraomnida.

Can we eat there?
거기서 식사할 수 있습니까?
keogiseo shiksahal su isseumnikka?

Of course, we can eat there.
물론 거기서 식사할 수 있습니다.
mulon geogiseo shiksahal su isseumnida.

Do we need tickets?
표가 있어야 합니까?
p'yoga isseoya hamnikka?

No, it's free.
아니요, 무료입니다.
aniyo, muryoimnida.

Tickets cost 5000 won each.

표는 한사람당 5000원입니다.

p'yoneun hansaramdang och'eonweon-imnida.

Where do we meet?

어디서 만납니까?

eo-di-seo mannamnikka?

In front of the hotel.

호텔앞에서요.

hot'elap'eseoyo.

How are we going to get there?

거기에 어떻게 갑니까?

keogi-e eotteoke gamnikka?

We are going by bus.

버스로 갑니다.

peoseu-ro gamnida.

(3) **At the Site**

What is the name of this place?

이곳은 이름이 무엇입니까?

igosseun ireum-i mueoshimnikka?

It's called _____.

이곳은 _____라고 합니다.

igosseun _____ rago hamnida.

When was this place built?

이곳은 언제 지어졌습니까?

igosseun eonje jieojyeosseumnikka?

It was built one hundred years ago.

이곳은 100년전에 지어졌습니다.

igosseun baengnyeonjeon-e jieo-jyeosseumnida.

May we go in?

들어가도 됩니까?

teureogado doimnikka?

Of course, you may.

물론 들어가도 됩니다.

mulon deureogado doimnida.

What is that place over there?

저너머는 이름이 무엇입니까?

cheoneomeoneun ireum-i mueoshimnikka?

May we take pictures?

사진을 찍어도 되나요?

sajineul jjig-eodo doinayo?

Will you please take my picture?

제 사진을 찍으시겠습니까?
che sajin-eul jjig-eu-shigesseumnikka?

What is this made of?
이것은 무엇으로 만들어졌나요?
igeosseun mueosseuro mandreojyeosseumnikka?

It's made of _____.
이것은 _____으로 만들어졌습니다.
igeosseun _____ euro mandreojyeosseumnida.

jade
구슬(guseul)

bronze
청동(ch'eongdong)

wood
목재(mokchae)

copper
구리(guri)

It's beautiful here.
이곳은 아름답습니다.
igosseun areumdapseumnida.

May we stay longer?
더 오래 머물 수 있나요.
deo orae meomul su innayo?

We must go back soon.
우리는 곧 돌아가야 합니다.

uri-neun got doragaya hamnida.

Can we buy a guide book?
안내책자를 살 수 있습니까?
annae ch'aekja-reul sal su isseumnikka?

Yes. It's very inexpensive.
네 그것은 매우 쌉니다.
ne geugeoseun maeu bissamnida.

We would like to come again.
우리 다시 오고 싶습니다.
uri dashi ogo shipseumnida.

This place is _____.
이곳은 _____입니다/습니다.
igoseun _____imnida/seumnida.

beautiful
아름다운(areunmdaun)

interesting
재미있는(chaemiinneun)

I am very tired.
나는 매우 피곤합니다.
naneun maeu p'igonhamnida.

I want to rest for a few minutes.
나는 몇분동안 쉬고 싶습니다.

naneun myeotpundong-an shigo shipseumnida.

Is there a bathroom here?

여기 화장실이 있습니까?

yeogi hwajangshil-i isseumnikka?

Please tell me where it is.

그것이 어데 있는지 말씀해 주세요.

keugeosi eode inneunji malsseumnhae jushipshio.

I would like to have a drink of water.

물한잔 먹고 싶습니다.

mulhanjan meog-go shipseumnida.

Thank you very much.

매우 감사합니다.

maeu gamsahamnida.

I had a wonderful time today.

오늘 정말 즐거운 시간이었습니다.

o-neul jeongmal jeulgeoun shigan-ieosseumnida.

(4) Pursuing individual interests

We're interested in _____.

우리는 _____ 에 관심있습니다.

urineun _____ e gwanshimisseumnida.

antiques	sculpture
골동품	조각
kolttongp'um	jogag

archeology	fine arts
고고학	미술
kogohag	misul

art	furniture
예술	가구
yesul	gagu

ceramics, pottery	Korean history
도자기	한국사
tojagi	hanguksa

arts and crafts	local carafts/products
미술공예품	지방토산물
misul gong-ye-pum	chibang t'osanmul

Korean painting	Korean music
한국화	한국 음악
hangug-hwa	hangug eum-ak

(5) Renting a car

There are a fair number of car rental services for visitors who wish to drive around the country. The rental fee ranges from about 50,000won to 10,000 won per day. Even if you are a good driver, you should remember that driving in any downtown areas is not like driving in your native country. Streets are always crowded with cars, taxis, buses, and pedestrians. So be prepared.

A lot of taxis are moving in the major cities throught downtown 24 hours. In Seoul and other cities you can rent a car easily. Taxis stop at designated taxi stands in front of department stores, hotels, railroad stations, and in certain areas downtown.

Taxis come in three different types; call taxi or hotel taxi, and kaein(individual) taxi. All of them have the meter showing the fare in digits. There is an initial charge 800 won for the first 2kilometers and about 50 won for each additional 400 meters. In case of heavy traffic, taxis are moving slowly or halts. Even in such cases fare is added to the initial fare.

The call taxi can be called by telephone anywhere in downtown Seoul and hotel taxis are available at most major hotels. Some drivers speak English fairly well. If you encounter a taxidriver who does not speak English, ask someone ahead of time to write down your destination in Korean.

I would like to rent a car.
차를 빌리고 싶습니다.

ch'areul biligo shipsseumnida.

How much will it cost to rent a car?
차빌리는 데 얼마나 듭니까?
cha' bilineun de eolmana deumnikka?

Do they provide a driver?
운전사가 딸립니까?
unjeonsaga ttalimnikka?

Does the driver speak English?
운전사가 영어로 말할 수 있나요?
unjeonsaga yeong-eoro malhal su innayo?

(6) Where is the _____ ?
Where is the _____ ?
    _____은 어디에 있습니까?
    _____ eun eodi-e isseumnikka?

palace 궁전(kungjeon)	university 대학(taehak)
statue 조각품(chogakp'um)	zoo 동물원(tongmulweon)
art gallery 미술관(misulgwan)	theatre 극장(keugjang)

handicrafts shop
미술공예품
(misulgong-yepum)

movie theatre
영화관
yeonghwagwan

center of town
도심지(toshimji)

ballet
발레(pale)

temple
절(cheol)

circus
서커스(seok'eoseu)

pavilion
정자(cheongja)

museum
박물관(pangmulgwan)

garden
화원(hwaweon)

shopping district
시장(shijang)

concert
음악회(eumakhoi)

lake
호수(hosu)

memorial monument
기념비(kinyeombi)

memorial hall
기념관(kinyeomgwan)

exhibition
전람회
cheonramhoi

opera house
국립도서관
kungrib doseogwan

(7) Is the _____ open today?

Is the _____ open today?

_____은 오늘 문을 열었습니까?

_____eun oneul munyeol-eosseumnikka?

Yes, it's open today.

네, 오늘 문 열었습니다.

ne, oneul mun yeoleosseumnida.

No, it's not open today.

아니요, 오늘 문열지 않았습니다.

aniyo, oneul munyeolji anasseumnida.

It opens at nine a.m. and closes at five p.m.

거기는 오전 아홉시에 열고 오후 다섯시에 닫습니다.

keogineun ojeon ahopshi-e yeolgo ohu daseosshi-e dasseumnida.

Is there an admission charge?

입장료가 있습니까?

ipch'angryoga isseumnikka?

There's no charge.

입장료는 없습니다.

ipchangryo-neun eopseumnida.

Is it far?

거리가 멉니까?

keoriga meomnikka?

Not at all. It's very close.

아니요, 매우 가깝습니다.

aniyo, maeu gakkapseumnida.

You can go by bus.

버스타고 갈 수도 있습니다.

peoseu t'ago galsudo isseumnida.

Please come with me.

나와 함께 갑시다.

nawa hamkke gapshida.

I would be happy to go with you.

당신과 함께 가게 되면 매우 기쁘겠습니다.

tangshin-gwa hamkke gage doemyeon maeu
gippeugesseumnida.

We have some free time tomorrow.

우리는 내일 여가가(시간이) 있습니다.

urineun naeil yeogaga(shjigan-i) isseumnida.

What shall we do for fun?

오락으로 무엇을 할까요?

orag-euro mueosseul halkkayo?

I would like to ____.
나는 ____하고 싶습니다.
naneun ____hago shipseumnida.

see a play
연극구경하다
yeongeug gugyeonghada.

go to the botanical gardens
식물원에 가다.
shingmulweon-e gada.

go to the park
공원에 가다
kongweon-e gada

go hear a concert
음악회에 가다
eum-ak-hoi-e gada

visit a ward(county) office
구(군)청에 가다
ku(kun)ch'eong-e gada.

go to the circus

서커스보러 가다
seokeoseu boreo gada

go to the zoo
동물원에 가다
tongmulweon-e gada

visit a factory
공장에 가다
kongjang-e gada

I don't want to go anywhere.
아무 곳에도 가고 싶지 않습니다.
amugossedo gago shipchi anseumnida.

I'm too tired.
나는 너무나 지쳤습니다.
na-neun neomuna jich'yeosseumnida.

I want to relax.
나는 쉬고 싶습니다.
na-neun suigo shipsseumnida.

(8) Useful Signs

Entrance	Exit
입구(ip-kku)	출구(ch'ul-gu)

East exit
동쪽 출구(tongjjok ch'ulgu)

Danger
위험(wi-heom)

West exit
서쪽출구(seojjok ch'ulgu)

Keep out
출입금지(ch'urip geumji)

South exit
남쪽출구(namjjok ch'ulgu)

Under construction
공사중(kongsajung)

Lavotory
공중변소(kongjung byeonso)

Fire extinguisher
소화기(sohwa-gi)

Elevator
승강기(seung-gang-gi)

Fee required
유료(yu-ryo)

Men
신사(shinsa)

Business hours
영업시간(yeong-eop shigan)

Women
숙녀(sungnyeo)

Closed hours
금일휴업(keum-il hyueop)

Adult
성인(seong-in)

Temporarily
임시휴업(imshi hyueop)

Child
어린이(eorin-i)

Staying open
야간영업(yagan yeongeop)

No smoking
금연(keumyeon)

Parking place
주차장(chuch'ajang)

No parking
주차금지(chuch'a geumji)

Waiting room
대기실(taegishil)

Hospital
병원(pyeong-weon)

Please ring
벨을 누르시오
pereul nureushio

Pull
당기시오(tang-gishio)

Push
미시오(mishio)

No entry
입장금지(ipchang geumji)

Caution
주의(chu-eui)

Emergency
비상구(pisang-gu)

Don't touch
손대지 마시오
sondaeji mashio

Information
안내소(annaeso)

Beware of dog
개주의(kaeju-eui)

Beware of fire
불조심(puljoshim)

Cashier
계산대(kyesandae)

For rent
세 놓음(se noeum)

No admittance
입장금지(ipchang geumji)

Private
개인용 (kaein-yong)

For sale
매품(mae-p'um)

Private property
사유지(sayuji)

Warning
경고(kyeong-go)

open
열었음(yeoreosseum)

Stop
중지(chung-ji)

Closed
닫았음(tadasseum)

Sold out
매진(mae-jin)

Out of order
고장
kojang

Don't drink the water
마시지 못함
mashiji mot'ham

Not in use
사용금지
sayong geumji

Shoes off
신을 벗으시오
shin-eul beoseushio

Fit for drinking
음료수(eumryosu)

Now in session
회의중(hoieui-jung)

Keep off the grass
잔디에 들어가지 마시오.
chandi-e deur-eo gaji mashio

(9) Visiting a family

Allow plenty of time to get to your destination because traffic is usually heavy since you are a stranger here. Don't wait for the last moment and then rush to your appointment.

Bring a small gift for the hostess when you are invited. Don't arrive empty-handed. When you are invited to a formal dinner, don't forget to take your invitation with you. You may have to present it when you arrive.

When arriving at any formal event, don't carry your coat into the main reception area. Check it with the cloakroom attendants. Wait till you've greeted the host and the guest of honor before having a drink.

When meeting people, Koreans usually exchange their calling cards after a firm handshake. Give your card only after you are introduced. But when you visit an office, give your card to the secretary or receptionist right away. Be careful not to sit just anywhere you want to, but wait to be offered a chair.

Here are some suggestions to make your visit more pleasant:

Good manners, patience, and courtesy are always in order.

Be on time for all activities.

I would like to invite you to dinner.
선생님을 저녁식사에 초대하고 싶습니다.
seonsaengnim-eul   jeonyeokshiksa-e   ch'odaehago
shipseumnida.

I'm very happy(to come). Thank you.
매우 기쁩니다. 감사합니다.
maeu gippeumnida. gamsahamnida.

What time shall we go?
몇시에 가나요?
myeoshi-e ganayo?

We'll go at 7:30.
일곱시 삼십분에 갈겁니다.
ilgopshi samshibun-e galgeomnida.

Where shall we meet?
우리 어디에서 만날까요?
uri eodieseo manalkkayo?

In front of the hotel.
호텔앞에서 (만납시다)
hot'elapeseo (mannabshida)

May I bring a friend?
친구를 데려갈까요?

ch'ingu-reul deryeo galkkayo?

Of course, you may.
물론 좋습니다.
mulon josseumnida.

Where shall we eat?
어디서 식사할까요?
eodiseo shiksahalkkayo?

Let's eat at a Lotte Hotel restaurant.
롯데호텔식당에서 식사합시다.
rottehot'el siktang eseo shiksahapshida.

(10) Adminstrative Divisions and Geographic Regions

city
시(shi)

myeon
면(myeon)

district
구(ku)

ri
리(ri)

dong(subdistrict)
동(tong)

province
도(to)

gun
군(kun)

region, area
지역/지방(chiyeok/chibang)

Kyeonggi Province
경기도(kyeonggido)

Kangwon Province
강원도(kangwondo)

N. Chungchong Province
충청북도
ch'ungch'eongbukdo

S. Chungchong Province
충청남도
ch'ungch'eongnamdo

S. Cholla Province
전라남도(jeolanamdo)

N. Cholla Province
전라북도(jeolabugdo)

S. Kyoungsang Province
경상남도
(kyeongsangnamdo)

N. Kyoungsang Province
경상북도
(kyeongsangbukdo)

Cheju Province
제주도(chejodo)

Kyeonggi Region
경기지역
(kyeonggijiyeok)

Kangwon Region
강원지역(kangwonjiyeok)

Chungchong Region
충청지역
ch'ungch'eongjiyeok

Honam Region
호남지역
honamjiyeok

Cheju Region
제주지역
(chejujiyeok)

7. Traveling

Most international flights to Korea arrive at Kimp'o International Airport which is about 42 kilometers away from the center of Seoul or about 50 minutes by taxi. Information on transportation or sightsseing are available at the airport information desk.

Tour groups within a city will often travel by tour buses, which are mostly comfortable and air—conditioned. Individual by the regular local bus is inexpensive and will give you a chance to use the phrases you've learned so far. If you plan to travel alone, it's a good idea to check with your guide first. Work out the details of your trip with him or her.

Taxis are available for both business and sightseeing, but they're quite expensive. You can arrange for a taxi with the help of your hotel service desk.

(1) By Airplane
I want to go to _____ by plane.
저는 비행기로 _____에 가고 싶습니다.
cheo-neun bihaeng-gi-ro_____e gago shipseumnida.

Pusan   Taegu
부산(pusan)   대구(taegu)

Jejudo
제주도(chejudo)

Ulsan
울산(ulssan)

Kwangju
광주(kwangju)

Kyeongju
경주(kyeongju)

Is there a plane to _____ ?
_____에 가는 비행기가 있습니까?
_____ e ganeun bihaenggi-ga isseumnikka?

Hongkong
홍콩
hongk'ong

Philippine
필리핀
p'ilip'in

Hawaii
하와이
hawa-i

Guam
구암
kuam

Australia
호주
hoju

When does the plane take off?
비행기가 언제 출발합니까?
P'ihaenggiga eonje ch'ulbalhamnikka?

Where can I buy a plane ticket?

비행기표를 어디서 살 수 있습니까?
pihaenggip'yoreul eodiseo salsu isseumnikka?

I want to buy two tickets to Pusan?
저는 부산행표 두장을 사고 싶습니다.
cheoneun busanhaengp'yo dujang-eul sago shipseumnida.

How much is the ticket price?
표값이 얼마입니까?
p'yogapshi eolmaimnikka?

Do you want a one-way ticket or a round-trip ticket?
편도표를 드릴까요 왕복표를 드릴까요.
p'yeondop'yo-rueul deurilkkayo wangbokp'yoreul
deurilkkayo?

One way ticket.
편도표입니다.
p'yeondop'yo-imnida.

Round-trip ticket.
왕복표입니다.
wangbokp'yo-imnida.

What time should I go to the airport?
공항에 몇시에 가야 합니까?

konghang-e myeossi-e gaya hamnikka?

Before two thirty.
두시삼십분전에요.
tushisamshippun-jeoneyo.

What is the flight number?
비행기는 몇번입니까?
pihaenggineun myeoppeon-imnikka?

Flight 262
이륙이번입니다.
i-ryug-i-beon-imnida.

What time do we arrive?
몇 시에 도착합니까?
myeoshi-e doch'akhamnikka?

We arrive at 6 p.m.
여섯시에 도착합니다.
yeoseossi-e doch'akhamnida.

Are you the stewardess?
당신이 스튜어디스입니까?
tangshin-i seuch'yueodiseu-imnikka?

Please help me with my bags.

가방을 좀 들어주십시오.
kabang-eul jom deur-eo-jushipshio.

Please help me.
도와주십시오.
dowajushipsio.

I don't feel well.
몸이 좋지 않습니다.
mom-i choch'i anseumnida.

I'm hungry.
저는 배가 좀 고픕니다.
cheoneun baega jom gop'eumnida.

Is there anything to eat.
먹을 것이 있나요?
meogeul kkeosi innayo?

I'm thirsty.
저는 목이 마릅니다.
cheoneun mog-i mareumnida.

I'd like some water.
물좀 마시고 싶습니다.
mul jom mashigo shipseumnida.

Where's the toilet?

화장실은 어디에 있습니까?

hwajangshil-eun eodi-e isseumnikka?

It's in the rear.

뒤에 있습니다.

dui-e isseumnida.

*Flying Times Between Major Cities

Seoul—Cheju	서울—제주	55minutes
Seoul—Pusan	서울—부산	50minutes
Seoul—Taegu	서울—대구	40minutes
Seoul—Kwangju	서울—광주	50minutes
Seoul—Ulsan	서울—울산	50minutes

(2) By Train

Traveling by train in Korea is very convenient and efficient. The railroad system operated by the Korean National Railroad has extensive connections from Seoul to most large cities.

Four types of trains can be employed for traveling as follows:

Special Express	Ordinary Express
특급열차	보통열차
t'eukkeup yeolch'a	pot'ong yeolch'a

Express
급행열차
keuphaeng yeolch'a

Local Train
구간열차
kugan yeolch'a

The special express has two classes of seats, first and second. Express, Ordinary Express, and Local trains have seats of second and third class. Seats on the first and second seats are reserved.

I want to reserve _____.
_____을 예약하고 싶습니다.
_____ eul yeyakhago shipseumnida.

first class seats
일등석
il-tteung-seok

second class seats
이등석
i-deung-seok

Is the train station far from here?
여기서 기차역이 멉니까?
yeogiseo gich'ayeog-i meomnikka?

It will only take a few minutes to get there.
거기까지 불과 몇분 안 걸립니다.
keogikkaji bulgwa myeoppun angeolimnida.

Where's the ticket office?
매표소는 어디에 있습니까?

maepyosoneun eodi-e isseumnikka?

It's over there.
저기에 있습니다.
cheogie isseumnida.

Is there a train for _____?
_____가는 기차 있습니까?
_____ganeun gich'a isseumnikka?

Yes. No. 네/아니오 ne/aniyo.

Please give me a time-table in English.
영어로 된 시간표 좀 주세요.
yeong-eoro doen shiganpyo jom juseyo.

I want to buy a ticket to Jeju.
제주행 표를 사고 싶습니다.
chejuhaeng p'yoreul sago shipseumnida.

How much is the fare?
요금은 얼마입니까?
yogeum-eun eolmaimnikka?

Twenty-five thousand won.
25,000원 입니다
iman och'eon won imnida.

At 4 : 00 p.m.

4시에 출발합니다.

neshi-e ch'ulbalhamnida.

Better hurry.

서두는게 좋겠어요.

seoduneung-ge jokkesseoyo.

The train will leave shortly!

기차가 바로 출발합니다.

kich'aga baro ch'ulbalhamnida.

Which track/platform?

몇번선로에서요?

myeoppeon seonroeseoyo?

Number five.

오번입니다.

obeon-imnida.

When is the next train?

다음 기차는 언제 있습니까?

taeum gich'a-neun eonje isseumnikka?

Please help me with my luggage.

짐을 나르는데 도와 주십시오.

chim-eul nareuneun de dowajushipshiyo.

All Aboard!

모두 타세요.

modu t'aseyo.

(3) By Car

Can I take a trip to Pusan by car?

부산까지 차로 갈 수 있습니까?

pusankkaji ch'aro gal su isseumnikka.

That is a very long trip.

매우 먼 여행입니다.

maeu meon yeohaeng-imnida.

How long will it take me?

제게는 얼마나 걸릴까요?

chege-neun nana geolilkkayo?

About one day.

약 하루요.

yak haruyo.

What can I see there?

거기서 무엇을 볼 수 있나요?

keogiseo mueosseul bol su innayo?

Are there many routes to take?

교통편이 거기에 많습니까?

kyot'ongp'yeon-i geogi-e mansseumnikka?

Can I see one of the national parks on the way?
가는 도중에 국립공원 하나를 볼 수 있나요?
kaneun dojung-e gungripkongweon hana-reul bol
su innayo?

Is Kyongju a wonderful city?
경주는 아름다운 도시인가요?
kyeongju-neun areumdaun doshi-ingayo?

It seems that Kyongju has everything.
경주에는 모든 게 다 있는 것 같아요.
kyeongjueneun modeun ge da inneun geo gat'ayo.

There is no place exactly like Kyongju in Korea.
한국에는 경주같은 곳이 없습니다.
hangugeneun gyeongjugat'eun goshi eopsseumnida.

＊Terms of Travel and Transportation

travel(ler)	tour(ist)
여행(자)	관광(객)
yeohaengja	kwan-gwang-gaek

airplane	airport
항공기, 비행기	공항
lang-gong-gi, piheng-gi	konghang

international airport	jet plane
국제공항	제트기
kugjegonghang	chet'eugi
international (air)line	domestic (air)line
국제선	국내선
kugjeseon	kungnaeseon
travel agency	customs
여행사	세관
yeohaengsa	segwan
reservation	tax
예약	세금
yeyag	segeum
passport	luggage, suitcase
여권	가방
yeogweon	kabang
visa	baggage, load
비자	짐
pija	chim
carry-on luggage	ship, boat
휴대품	선박, 배
hyudaep'um	seonbag, pae

train	passenger boat
기차, 열차	여객선
kich'a, yeolch'a	yeogaegseon
freight, cargo	subway
화물	지하철
hoamul	chihach'eol
cargo ship	bus
화물선	버스
hoamulseon	beoseu
freight car(train)	express bus
화물열차	고속버스
hoamulyeolch'a	kosogbeoseu
express(high) way	taxi
고속도로	택시
kosokttoro	t'aekshi
car	fare
차/자동차	요금
ch'a/chadongch'a	yeogeum
truck	rest area
트럭	휴식처
teureog	hyushikch'eo

restroom
화장실
hwajangshil

shop, store
상점
sangjeom

(4) Major Holidays

January 1
New Year's day
양력설(신정)
yangryeog-seol

1st day of lunar January
Folklore Day
음력설(구정)
eumryeokseol(kujeong)

March 1
Independence Movement Day
삼일절
sam-il jjeol

April 5
Labor Day
식목일
shingmog-il

May 5
Children's Day
어린이날
eorini-nal

8th day of 4th
Buddha's Birthday
석가탄신일
seokka t'anshin-il

July 17
Constitution Day
제헌절
cheheon-jeol

June 6
Memorial Day
현충일
hyeonch'ung-il

August 15
Liberation Day
광복절
kwangbok-cheol

15th day of 8th(lunar)
Ch'useok
추석
ch'useok

October 3
National Foundation Day
개천절
kaech'eon-jeol

Octorber 9
Korean Alphabet Day
한글날
hangeul nal

December 25
Christmas
성탄절
seongt'an-jeol

(5) Major Cities

Seoul	서울	Pyongtaek	평택
Inchon	인천	Taegu	대구
Anyang	안양	Pusan	부산
Suwon	수원	Ulsan	울산
Masan	마산		
Mokpo	목포	Taejon	대전
Kwangju	광주	Onyang	온양
Chonju	전주	Chunchon	춘천
		Chongju	청주
Wonju	원주	Kangnung	강릉
Socho	속초		

〈지도삽입〉

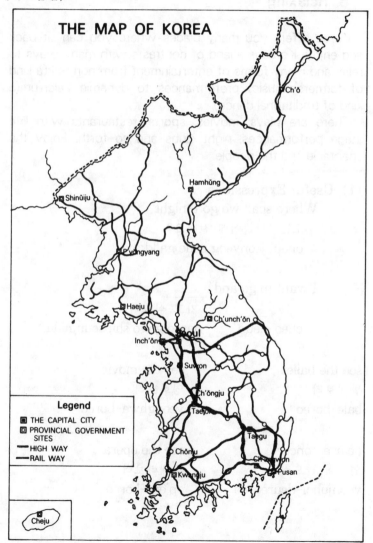

THE MAP OF KOREA

Ch'ŏ

Hamhŭng

Shinŭiju

P'yŏngyang

Haeju

Ch'unch'ŏn

Inch'ŏn

Seoul

Suwŏn

Ch'ŏngju

Taejŏn

Taegu

Chŏnju

Ch'angwŏn

Kwangju

Pusan

Legend

THE CAPITAL CITY

PROVINCIAL GOVERNMENT SITES

HIGH WAY

RAIL WAY

Cheju

8. Relaxing

Korea offers you many places where you can sit back and enjoy. Korea is a land of contrasts with many ways to relax and many forms of entertainment from nong-ak(a kind of farmers' music) preformances to dynamic t'alch'um(a kind of tradititonal dance).

There are plays, movies, sports, restaurants with live stage performances, night clubs and so forth. Enjoy the spectacle and the people.

(1) Useful Expressions

Where shall we go tonight?

오늘 저녁 어데 갈까요?

oneul jeonyeog eode galkkayo?

I want to go and _____.

저는 _____하러 가고 싶습니다.

cheo-neun ____hareo gago shipseumnida.

see the ballet	see the movie
발레보러	영화보러
bale-boreo	yeonghwa-boreo
hear a concert	see the opera
연주회 들으러	오페라보러
yeonjuhoi-deureureo	op'era-boreo

see a Korean movie
한국영화보러
hanggug-yeonghwa-boreo

see a foreign movie
외국영화보러
oigugyeonghwa-boreo

go to a bar
술집에
suljib-e

go to a nightclub
나이트클럽에
naitk'euleob-e

go to a restaurant.
식당에
shikttang-e

see the circus
서커스 보러
seok'eoseu-boreo

see a sporting event
스포츠 경기보러
sp'otskyong-gi-boreo

How should I dress?
어떻게 옷을 입을까요?
eotteokke osseul ibeulkkayo?

Any sort of clothes will do.
어떤옷도 괜찮습니다.
eotteon otto kwaen ch'anseumnida.

What movie is showing today?

오늘 어떤 영화가 상연되나요?

oneul eo-tteon yeonghwa-ga sang-yeon-doinayo?

What time does it start?

몇시에 시작하나요?

myeoshi-e shijakhanayo?

What time does it end?

몇시에 끝나나요?

myeoshi-e kkeunnanayo?

Do we need tickets?

표를 사야 되나요?

p'yo reul saya doinayo?

Please call a taxi.

택시좀 불러주십시오.

t'aekshi-jom buleojushipsio.

I want to go to ____.

저는 ____에 가고 싶습니다.

cheo-neun ____e gago shipseumnida.

Good enening, My name is ____.

안녕하세요, 저는 ____입니다.

annyeong-haseyo? cheo-neun ____imnida.

I have already reserved a table.
제가 벌써 테이블을 예약했습니다.
chega beolseo t'eibeul-eul yeyakhaesseumnida.

Is food served here?
음식이 여기서 제공되나요?
eumshigi yeogiseo jegongdoenayo?

Can we buy drinks?
음료도 살수 있나요?
eumryodo sal su innayo?

(2) Making friends

How do you do.
처음뵙겠습니다.
ch'eo-eum boibkkesseumnida.

How are you!
안녕하세요?
annyeonghaseyo?

My name is ____.
제 이름은 ____입니다.

che ireum-eun ____ imnida.

I'm an American.

저는 미국인입니다.

cheoneun migug-in imnida.

I'm a foreigner.

저는 외국인입니다.

cheo-neun oigug-inimnida.

What's your name?

당신의 이름은 무엇입니까?

tangshin-eui ireum-eun mueoshimikka?

May I introduce ____ ?

____를 소개할까요?

____ reul sogaehalkkayo?

I would like to meet a friend of mine.

제 친구를 만나보셨으면 좋겠습니다.

che ch'ingu-reul mannabosyeosseumyeon jokkesseumnida.

This is _____.

이 사람은 ____입니다.

isarameun ____imnida.

How long have you been in Korea?
한국에 얼마나 계셨습니까?
hangug-e eolmana gyeseosseumnikka?

I've been here about two weeks.
약 2주쯤 있었습니다.
yag i-jujjeum isseosseimmida.

Are you enjoying yourself?
재미있는 시간을 보내고 있습니까?
chaemi-inneun shiganeul bonaego isseumnikka?

We're very busy.
우리는 매우 바쁩니다.
uri-neun maeu bappeumnoda.

Did you come alone?
혼자 오셨습니까?
honja oshyeosseumnikka?

my wife (나의 아내)   my family (나의 가족)
naeui ane   naeui gajok

my parents (나의부모)
naeui bumo

9. Communicating

Everwhere you will see payphone booths where you can either use coins (10, 50, 100 denominations) or your plastic card. From a public booth you may call overseas, see your hotel clerk or ask a friend since rates for such are rather high.

Local calls cost 20 won, is very cheap when compared with other countries. Long-distance calls also possible by public telephone calls if you have a plastic phone card.

If you plan to call home, remember that Korean time is different.

(1) Making a call

Is there a telephone here?

여기 전화기 있습니까?

yeogi jeonhwagi isseumnikka?

May I use the phone?

전화 좀 써도 됩니까?

cheonhwa jom sseodo doimnikka?

Please help me make a telephone call.

전화거는 데 좀 도와주세요.

cheonhwageoneunde jom dowajuseyo.

I want to make a phone call to ____ .

___에게 전화하고 싶습니다.
___ege jeonhwa-hago shipseumnida.

My friend, Mr.Smith   a Korean restaurant
나의 친구 스미스씨   한국식당
naeui ch'ingu seumiseussi   hanguk shikttang

the American Embassy   the hotel
미국대사관   호텔
migug daesagwan   hot'el

How do I make a long distance call?
장거리 전화를 어떻게 합니까?
changeori jeonhwa-reul eotteoke hamnikka?

Please go to the service desk to handle it.
담당 안내역한테로 가세요.
tamdang annaeyeog-hant'ero gaseyo.

(2) In the street
Can you speak English?
영어를 하십니까?
yeong-eo-reul hashimnikka?

What?

뭐라구요?
mueoraguyo?

I know very little English.
영어를 조금 압니다.
yeong-eoruel jogeum ammnida.

What did you say?
뭐라고 말씀하셨습니까?
mueorago malsseumhasyeosseumnikka?

Is there anyone who speaks English?
영어를 말하는 사람 있습니까?
yeong-eo-reul malhaneun saram isseumnikka?

Speak slowy, please.
좀 천천히 말씀해 주십시오.
chom ch'eonch'eonhi malsseumhae jushipshiyo.

Do you understand?
아시겠습니까?
ashigesseumnikka?

No, I don't understand.
아니요 모르겠습니다.

aniyo, moreugesseumnida.

Excuse me, could you help me.
실례합니다. 저 좀 도와주시겠습니까?
shillyehamnida jeo jom dowajushigesseumnikka?

Please say it again.
다시 좀 말씀해 주십시요.
tashi chom malsseumhae jushipshio.

Who is that?
저 분은 누구십니까?
cheobuneun nugushimnikka?

Pardon me, may I introduce myself?
실례지만 저를 소개해도 되겠습니까?
sillyejiman jeoreul sogaehaedo doigesseumnikka?

How do you do?
처음 뵙겠습니다.
ch'eoeum boepkesseumnida.

I'm glad to see you.
만나서 반갑습니다.
mannaseo bangapseumnida.

I would like to meet him.

그분을 만나보고 싶습니다.

keubun-eul manabogo shipseumnida.

My name is Michael.

저는 마이클입니다.

cheoneun maikeulimnida.

Would you introduce me to him?

저를 그분에게 소개해주시겠습니까?

jeoreul guebunege sogaehae jushigesseumnikka?

May I have your card?

선생님의 명함을 좀 주시겠습니까?

seonsaengnim-eui myeonghameul jom jushige
sseumnika?

Here's my card.

제 명함입니다.

che myeongham-imnida.

Where are you from?

어디서 오셨습니까?

eodiseo osyeosseumnikka?

Are you from _____?

_____에서 오셨습니까?

_____eseo osyeosseumnikka?

I'm from _____.

저는 _____에서 왔습니다.

cheoneun _____eseo oassseumnida.

How long will you be here?

얼마동안 여기에 계시겠습니까?

eolma-dong-an yeogi-e gyeshigesseumnikka?

Where are you staying?

어디에 머물고 있습니까?

eodi-e meomulgo isseumnikka?

Where can I call you?

어디로 연락하면 됩니까?

eodi-ro yeollakhamyeon doimnikka?

Here's my address and phone number.

제 주소와 전화번호입니다.

je juso-wa jeonhwa-beonho-imnida.

Thanks a lot.

대단히 고맙습니다.
taedanhi gomapsseumnida.

Can you pick me up tomorrow morning?
내일 아침 저를 태워줄실 수 있습니까?
naeil ach'im jeo-reul taeweojushil su isseumnikka?

See you tomorrow morning.
내일 아침에 봅시다.
naeil ach'im-e bopshida.

See you later.
조금 후에 만납시다.
ch'oguem hu-e mannapshida.

PART III
FOR BUSINESS TRAVELERS

Businessmen always try to seek our new markets for their products, to develop more efficient ways to distribute or sell their goods to more people. So they often travel to foreign countries where language and customs are different. Even when a businessman knows the Korean language, the specialized and often idiosyncratic terminology of the business world can be an obstacle to successful negotiations. Here is an essential pocket reference for all business travellers to Korea. Whether your business is manufacturing or finance, communications or sales, this part will put the right words in your mouth and the best possible expressions in your correspondence.

1. Business Customs in Koera

Korea also has its peculiarities with respect to customs and culture. Over the past centuries Confucianism has exerted a great deal of influence on Korean mores. In many instances, manners and life styles are quite different from those of Western countries, One may say that business is a matter of sentiment. That is why businessmen should understand the culltural background when doing business with Koreans. In this vein, the following points will prove useful to you as you try to develop a successful business transaction.

① Learn how to use chopsticks, Once accustomed to using them, you will find them coming handy both as a means of picking food and showing off your dexterity at handling an odd custom of your host or hostess.

② Should you want to conduct serious business negotiations, meet your counterpart in Persons. Like other people whose cultures are rooted in oral tradition, Koreans prefer to talk in person rather than by phone or written correspondence about matters that require sure comprehension and hard thinking.

③ When entering someone's home, be sure to take your shoes off. This unwritten rule should be observed especially when you enter a home with ondol floor, And this is a custom still in effect throughout the country. Remember the fact that Koreans as any other people want to keep their room always clean in any case.

④ Beware that Koreans in general do not like to make an eye-to-eye contact all the time when engaged in a conversation because to them it sometimes implies impolilteness or rudness.

⑤ Never write any personal names or even short memos in red ink because it is considered sinister. Red ink is used only when you stamp your tojang(the chop of seal) on documents.

⑥ Also beware that Koreans always say or write their

surnames (or family names) first, then the given name followed by a suitable honorific title such as "seonsaeng-nim"
(meaning "Mr" or "Sir") and other formal titles (see the
common business terms, plus the "Cure-all" suffix indicating
respect "nim".)

⑦ For reasons of trust building, it is usually good idea for
you to be introduced to government officials or company
representatives through a friend of yours or someone you
already know.

⑧ A trip to a bar or a restaurant usually means an exten-
sion of busness although at times the substance of your
talk may not be explicitly related to business.

⑨ If you don't know how to behave in some cases, you
can ask or use any good Western manners.

⑩ You don't need to show gratitude at hotel because all
costs are already included in your bill.

⑪ Sometimes it is effective to be introduced to officals
through your acquaintance in order to maintain a positive re-
lationship with him.

⑫ If Koreans take you to a bar or restaurant, it is usually a
part of business.

(1) Business Meeting

Hello. Good morning.

안녕하십니까?

annyong-hashimnikka?

How do you do?

처음뵙겠습니다.

ch'eoeum beop-kesseumnida.

What's your name?

성함이 어떻게 되십니까?

seongham-i eotteok'e doe-shimmnikka?

I am_____.

저는 _____입니다.

cheo-neun_____imnida.

Do you speak English?

영어를 하십니까?

yeong-eo-reul hashimnikka?

I speak a little Korean.

한국말을 조금 합니다.

hanggugmal-eul jogeum hamnida.

What did you say?

뭐라고 말씀하셨습니까?

mueorago malsseum-hasyeosseumnikka?

Please repeat it slowly.
다시 천천히 말씀해주십시오.
tashi ch'eonch'eonhi malsseum-hae jushipshiyo.

Excuse me. What does this mean?
실례지만 이것이 무슨 뜻입니까?
shilyejiman, igeoshi museun tteushimnikka?

I don't understand.
저는 모르겠습니다.
cheo-neun moreu-gesseumnida.

It doesn't matter.
괜찮습니다.
kwaench'an-sseumnida.
상관없습니다.
sang-guan eopseumnida.

Where are the restrooms?
화장실이 어디 있습니까?
hwajangshir-i eodi isseumnikka?

Would you call me a cab, please?
택시좀 불러 주시겠습니까?
t'aekshi jom buleo-jushigesseumnikka?

Thank you very much.
대단히 감사합니다.
taedanhi gamsa-hamnida.

What time is it?
지금 몇시입니까?
chigeum myeoshi-imnikka?

Good-bye.
안녕히 가십시오.
annyeonghi ga-shipshiyo.

(2) Telegrams and Telexes

Where do I go to send_____?
_____보내러 어디로 가야 합니까?
_____bonaereo eodiro gaya hamnikka?

a telegram
전보(cheonbo)

a cable
해외(전보)(haeoe jeonbo)

a telex
텔렉스(t'elekseu)

a fax
팩스(p'aeks)

Does the hotel have a telex machine?
호텔에 텔렉스가 있습니까?
hot'el-e telekseu-ga isseumnikka?

How late is it open?

얼마나 늦게까지 문을 엽니까?

eolmana neukkekkaji mun-eul yeomnikka?

I'd like to send a telegram to_____.

_____로 전보를 보내고 싶습니다.

_____ro jeonboreul bonaego shipsseumnida.

What is the cost per_____?

_____에 얼마나 듭니까?

_____e eolmana deumnikka?

per minute	per word
일분당(ilbun-dang)	한단어 당(handan-eo-dang)

Where are the forms?

양식이 어디에 있습니까?

yangshig—i eodi—e isseumnikka?

Please give me a form.

양식을 하나 주세요.

yangshik-eul hanajuseyo.

I want to send it collect.

수취인 부담으로 보내고 싶습니다.

such'ue-in budameuro bonaego shipsseumnida.

When will it arrive?

언제쯤 도착할까요?

eonjejjeum doch'akhalkkayo?

Is my writing clear?

제 글씨가 분명합니까?

je-geulssiga bunmyeonghamnikka?

Do you normally deliver telexes to guest rooms?

객실에 보통 전보를 보냅니까?

kaekshil-e bot'ong jeonboreul bonaemnikka?

(3) At the Lodging

Do you have any messages for me?

저한테 무슨 연락온 것 있습니까?

cheo-hant'e museun yellag-on geot isseumnikka?

Is the barber still open?

이발소가 아직도 열려 있습니까?

ibalso-ga ajigdo yeolyeo isseumnikka?

Where can I buy English-language newspapers?

영자신문을 어데서 살 수 있습니까?

yeongjja shimmun-eul eodiseo sal su isseumnikka?

(4) Looking for Help

I'm lost.

길을 잃었습니다.

kireul ireosseumnida.

Where is the post office?

우체국이 어디에 있습니까?

uch'egug-i eodi-e isseumnikka?

And the mailbox?

우체통은요?

uch'etong-eun yo?

I would like to make a phone call.

전화걸고 싶습니다.

cheonhwa-geolgo shipseumnida.

2. Banking

Banking services are available in many places in Korea. Traveler's checks are accepted and can be converted easily. Double check with your travel agency to make sure your particular traveler's checks will be accepted. Carry your passport when you do your banking. Keep records of all your currency exchanges. Remember that you must declare your foreign currency.

The official name for Korean currency is won, The bank notes come in 100,500,1,000, 5,000 and 10,000 won denominations; coins in 10, 50, 100, and 500 won denominations.

The exchange rate is subject to change depending on the daily flutuations of the foreign money market, although the won is closely tied to the U. S. dollar. The current exchange rate is about 790 won to the U.S. dollar, as of the early of August, 1992. Information about the current exchange rates is available at banks, tourist offices, and hotels.

(1) Basic Words

ten thousand won
만원
manweon

five thousand won
오천원
och'eonweon

one thousand won
천원
ch'eonweon

five hundred won
오백원
obaegweon

one hundred won(coins)	fifty won(coins)
백원	오십원
paegweon	oshibweon
ten won(coins)	one hundred dollars/pounds
십원	백달러/파운드
shibweon	paekttaleo/p'aundeu
three dollars	forty cents
삼달러	사십센트
sam-ttaleo	saship-senteu
twenty five cents	five cents
이십오센트	오센트
iship-osenteu	o-senteu

(2) To the Bank

Where's the bank?

은행이 어디에 있습니까?

eunhaeng-i eodi-e isseumnikka?

The nearest is on _____ street.

가장 가까운 것은_____거리/로에 있습니다.

kajang kakkaun geoseun_____geori/ro-e isseumnida.

What time does it open?

몇시에 문을 엽니까?

myeotshi-e mun-eul yeomnikka?

It open at nine a.m.

9시에 엽니다.

ahopshi-e yeomnida.

It closes at 4 p.m.

4시에 닫습니다.

neshi-e dasseumnida.

Is it open Saturday, also?

토요일에도 여나요?

t'oyoil-edo yeonayo?

Yes, it is.

네, 그렇습니다.

Ne, keureosseumnida.

(3) Office in the City

Where can I exchange American dollars?

어디서 미국달러를 바꿀 수 있나요?

eodiseo miguk daleo-reul bakkul su innayo?

Where can I exchange Hong Kong dollars?

어디서 홍콩달러를 바꿀 수 있나요?

eodiseo hongk'ong daleo-reul bakkul su innayo?

Where can I exchange British pounds?

호텔에서 돈을 바꿀 수 있습니다.

hotel-eseo don-eul pakkul su isseumnida.

I want to cash a Traveler's Check.

여행자 수표를 바꾸고 싶습니다.

yeohaengja supyo-reul bakkugo shipseumnida.

Go to that clerk, please.

저분한테 가세요.

cheobun-hant'e kasseyo.

How much do you want to exchange?

얼마나 바꾸시겠어요?

eolmana bakkushigesseoyo?

Fifty dollars.

50달러요.

oshipttaleo-yo.

May I see your passport?

여권 좀 보여 주시겠어요?

yeokweon jom boyeo jushigesseoyo?

Here is my passport.

여기 제 여권이 있습니다.

yeogi je yeokkweon-i isseumnida.

Will you accept traveler's checks?

여행자수표를 받으시겠어요?

yeohaengja supyo-reul badeushigeseoyo?

Yes(I/we do).

네 받습니다.

ne, basseumnida.

Can you cash a personal check?

자기앞 수표도 바꾸어 주나요?

chagiap-supyodo bakku-eo junayo.

Do you have any personal I.D.?

신분증을 가지고 계세요?

shinbunjeung-eul gajigo kyeseyo?

Yes, I have a passport.

네, 여권이 있습니다.

ne, yeokweon-i isseumnida.

Please sign here.

여기 사인좀 해주세요.

yeogi sain jom hae-juseyo.

Who speaks English here?

여기서 누가 영어를 말합니까?

yeogiseo nuga yeong-eo reul malhamnikka?

Can you telex my bank in the United States?

미국에 있는 제 거래은행에 텔렉스 보낼 수 있습니까?

migug-e inneun je eunhaeng-e t'elelkseu boanel su isseumnikka?

I have a letter of introduction.

저는 소개장이 있습니다.

cheoneun sogaejang-i isseumnida.

Please give me 100 dollars in Korean currency.

100달러좀 원화로 바꾸어주세요.

paekttaleo jom weonhwa-ro bakkueo juseyo.

Please count it to see if it is correct.

맞는지 세어 보세요.

manneunji seeo boseyo.

Will you please sign this receipt?

이 영수증에 사인 좀 해주세요.

i yeongsujeung-e sain jom hae juseyo.

Here's your change.

여기 거스름 돈이 있습니다.

yeogi keoseureum don-i isseumnida.

I want to open a bank account.

은행구좌를 트고 싶습니다.

eunhaengkwjoareul t'eugo shipsseumnida.

I would like to deposit some money.

돈을 좀 예금하고 싶습니다.

doneul jom yekeumhago shipsseumnida.

Which form do I use?

어떤 용지에 써야 하나요?

eotteon yongji-e sseoya doenayo.

Where do I sign?

어디에 사인해야 되나요?

eodi-e sainhaeya doenayo.

What is the exchange rate today?

오늘 환율은 얼마인가요?

oneul howanryul-eun eolmain-gayo?

(4) Name of Banks and Related Terms

Bank of Korea

한국은행

hangguk-eunhaeng

Foreign Exchange Bank

외환은행

oihwan-eunhaeng

City Bank

시티은행

shit'i-eunhaeng

Industrial Bank of Korea

중소기업은행

chungsogieob-eunhaeng

Commercial Bank

상업은행

sang-eob-eunhaeng

head office

본점

ponjeom

Korea-America Bank

한미은행

hanmi-eunhaeng

Trust Bank

신탁은행

shint'ag-eunhaeng

Chief of Branch	President of Bank
지점장	은행장
chijeom-jang	eunhaeng-jang
branch	check
지점	수표
chijeom	sup'yo
insurance	personal check
보험	자기앞수표
poheom	chagiap sup'yo
window	deposit
창구	예금
ch'ang-gu	ye-geum
withdraw	cash
대출	현금
taech'ul	hyeon-geum
insurance company	contract(document)
보험회사	계약(서)
p'oheom-hoesa	kyeyakseo

sales contact	ownership, title
판매계약	소유권
pa'nmae-gyeyak	soyu-gweon
sales dept.	advertising dept.
판매부	광고부
p'anmae-bu	kwang-go-bu
business dept.	
사업부	
sa-eob-bu	

(5) Titles of Businessmen/women

chairman	president
회장(hoejang)	사장(sajang)
vice president	executive director
부사장(pusajang)	전무(cheonmu)
director	division chief
상무(sangmu)	부장(pujang)
bureau chief	deputy chief
국장(kukjang)	차장(ch'ajang)

head of department	section
과장(kwajang)	실장(shiljang)

assistant head	unit leader
대리(taeri)	계장(kyejang)

board member	board of directors
이사(isa)	이사진(isajin) *

board chairman
이사장(isajang)

Note that all these titles except the one marked are usually followed by the honorific affix "nim" especially in a face-to face situation where a measure of formality is necessary.

3. Useful Words for Business

abstract of title
권리증서
kweolli jeungseo

account
구좌
kujwa

account balance
구좌잔고
kujwa jan-go

account period
거래기간
keorae gigan

adjusted CIF price
운임-보험료 포함조정가격
unim boheomryo p'oham
jo-jeong gagyeok

advance notice
사전통고
sajeon t'ong-go

advertising agency
광고대행업
kwang go daehaeng-eop

afterdate(V)
후불하다(hubul-hada)

agency
대리점(taerijeom)

approved securities
공인유가증권
kong-in yuga jeungkkweon

aggregate demand
총수요(ch'ongsuyo)

arbitrage
중개거래
chung-gae georae

associate company
동업자 회사
tongeopjja hoesa

at par
액면 그대로
aengmyeon geudaero

at the market
시장가격으로
shijang gagyeog-euro

at the opening
개장시
kaejangshi

attestation
증명서
cheungmyeongseo

authorized dealer
공인중개사
kong-in junggaesa

average price
평균가격
p'yeong-gyun gagyeok

back date
연체일
yeonch'e-il

balance of payments
국제수지
kukche suji

balance of trade
무역수지
muyeog suji

balance
은행잔고
eunhaeng jan-go

bank deposit
은행예금
eunhaeng yegeum

bankruptcy
파산
p'asan

barter
물물교환하다
mulmul gyohwan-hada

below par
액면이하로
aengmyeoniha-ro

bid
입찰
ipch'al

blue chip stock
우량주식
uryang jushik

business management
사업경영
sa-eop kyeong-yeong

bill of exchange
환어음
hwan-eoeum

capital market
자본시장
chabon shijang

cable transfer
전신환
cheonshinhwan

capital, working
운영자본
unyeong jabon

capital surplus
자본잉여금
chabon ing-yeogum

cash delivery
현금인도
hyeon-geum indo

cash in advance
선불
seonbul

ceiling
상한선
sanghanseon

charge account
외상거래 계정
oesang-georae gyejeong

chief executive
최고 경영인
ch-oego gyeongyeong-in

colleague
동업자
tong-eobja

carnet
무관세 허가증
mugwanse heogajjung

cashier's check
자기앞 수표
chagi-ap sup'yo

certified public accountant
공인회계사
kong-in hoegyesa

checklist
대조표
taejop'yo

classified ad.
구직광고
kujik kjwang-go

commercial bank
상업은행
sangeob-eunhaeng

commodity exchange
상품거래소
sangp'um georae so

composite index
종합지수
chonghab jisu

consolidation
합병
happyeong

consumer goods
소비재
sobijae

consumer price
소비자 물가
sobija mulkka

corporation tax
법인세
peobinse

cost
원가
weonkka gyesan

cost analysis
원가계산
weonkka gyesan

cost, indirect
간접비
kanjeoppi

credit bank
신용대부 은행
shinyong daebu eunhaeng

creditor
채권자
ch'aekkweonja

deadline
준비금 한계선
junbigeum han-gyesseon

deed
증서
cheungseo

department store
백화점
paekhwajeom

depository
금고
keumgo

discount
할인
harin

entrepreneur
사업가
saeopkka

factor
대리점
taerijeom

fiduciary issue
신용발행
shinyong balhaeng

fixed costs
고정비용
kojeong biyong

footing
합계
hapkkye

foreign exchange
외국환
oegukhwan

goods
상품
sang'pum

holder
주주
chuju

gross profit
총이익
ch'ong i-ik

impulse buying
충동구매
ch'ungdong gumae

indirect tax
간접세
kanjeop-se

inflation
통화팽창
t'onghwa p'aengch'ang

insurance broker
보험 중개인
poheom jung-gaein

incom tax
소득세
sodeukse

income, net
순소득
sun-sodeuk

index option
주가 지수
chukka jisu

insolvent
지불불능의
chibul bulneung-eui

PART V
NUMBERS AND OTHERS

You will use numbers the moment you arrive in Korea, whether it be to exchange money at the airport, pay a taxi driver, or describe the length of your stay to a customs official or hotel clerk. Followings are the frequently used cardinal and ordinal numbers, and also for specifying fractions and other useful measures.

Koreans use two kinds of numerals, one of Korean origin and the other of chinese origin. Chinese origin. Chinese numerals are generally used on money matters, the metric system, and counting floors of a building, minutes and seconds of the clock, hours, days, months and years. Here we begin with cardinal numbers.

(1) Counting Numbers

1) Cardinal Numbers

	Korean Origin		Chinese Origin	
0	영	yeong	영	yeong
1	하나	hana	일	il
2	둘	tul	이	i
3	셋	set	삼	sam
4	넷	net	사	sa
5	다섯	taseot	오	o
6	여섯	yeoseot	육	yuk
7	일곱	ilgop	칠	ch'il

8	여덟	yeodeol	팔	p'al
9	아홉	ahop	구	ku
10	열	yeol	십	ship
11	열하나	yeol−hana	십일	shibil
12	열둘	yeolttul	십이	shibi
13	열셋	yeol−set	십삼	shibsam
14	열넷	yeol−net	십사	shipsa
15	열다섯	yeol−ttaseot	십오	shibo
16	열여섯	yeol−yeoseot	십륙	shimnyuk
17	열일곱	yeol−ilgop	십칠	shipch'il
18	열여덟	yeol−yeodeol	십팔	shipp'al
19	열아홉	yeol−ahop	십구	shibgu
20	스물	seumul	이십	iship
30	서른	seoreun	삼십	samship
40	마흔	maheun	사십	saship
50	쉰	swin	오십	oship
60	예순	yesun	육십	yukship
70	일흔	irheun	칠십	ch'ilship
80	여든	yeodeun	팔십	p'alship
90	아흔	aheun	구십	kuship
99	아흔아홉	aheun−ahop	구십구	kushipgu

Up to 99 both numerals are used interchangeably, How-ever, from 100 on, Chinese numerals are used almost exclusively.

100	(일)백	(il)baek
200	이 백	ibaek
300	삼 백	sambaek
400	사 백	sabaek
500	오 백	obaek
600	육 백	yukbaek
700	칠 백	ch'ilbaek
800	팔 백	p'albaek
900	구 백	kubaek
1000	(일)천	(il)ch'eon
2000	이 천	ich'eon
3000	삼 천	samch'eon
4000	사 천	sach'eon
5000	오 천	och'eon
6000	육 천	yukch'eon
7000	칠 천	ch'ilch'eon
8000	팔 천	p'alch'eon
9000	구 천	kuch'eon
10,000	(일)만	(il)man
20,000	이 만	iman
30,000	삼 만	samman
40,000	사 만	saman
50,000	오 만	oman
60,000	육 만	yungman
70,000	칠 만	ch'ilman
80,000	팔 만	p'alman
90,000	구 만	kuman

100,000	(일)십만	(il)shimman
200,000	이십만	ishimman
300,000	삼십만	samshimman
400,000	사십만	sashimman
500,000	오십만	oshimman
600,000	육십만	yukshimman
700,000	칠십만	ch'ilshimman
800,000	팔십만	p'alshimman
900,000	구십만	kushimman
1000,000	(일)백만	ilbaengman
2000,000	이백만	ibaengman
3000,000	삼백만	sambaengman
4000,000	사백만	sabaengman
5000,000	오백만	obaengman
6000,000	육백만	yukbaengman
7000,000	칠백만	ch'ilbaengman
8000,000	팔백만	p'albaengman
9000,000	구백만	kubaengman
10,000,000	(일)천만	(il)ch'eonman
20,000,000	이천만	ich'eonman
30,000,000	삼천만	samch'eonman
100,000,000	(일)억	(ir)eok
1,000,000,000	십억	shibeok
10,000,000,000	백억	paegeok
100,000,000,000	천억	ch'eoneok
1,000,000,000,000	조	cho

e.g.

307	삼백칠
	sambaekch'il
2,549	이천오백사십구
	ich'eon-obaek-sa-ship-ku
33,654	삼만삼천육백오십사
	samman-samch'eon-yukbaeg-oshipsa
1,642,350	백육십사만이천삼백오십
	baek-yukshipsaman-ich'eonsambaeg-oship

2) Ordinal Numbers

Making cardinal numbers into ordinal numbers is a simple task in the Korean language, You simply add the suffix (bbeon)jjae, Note the following examples :

Korean ordinal numbers

first	second
첫(번)째	두(번)째
ch'eot(bbeon)jjae	tu(bbeon)jjae

third	forth
세(번)째	네(번)째
se(bbeon)jjae	ne(bbeon)jjae

fifth
다섯(번)째
taeo(bbeon)jjae

sixth
여섯(번)째
yeoseot(bbeon)jjae

seventh
일곱(번)째
ilgop(bbeon)jjae

eighth
여덟(번)째
yeodeol(bbeon)jjae

ninth
아홉(번)째
ahob(bbeon)jjae

tenth
열(번)째
yeol(bbeon)jjae

Chinee ordinal numbers

first (제일)
che-il

second (제이)
che-i

third (제삼)
che-sam

forth (제사)
che-sa

fifth (제오)
che-o

sixth (제육)
che-yuk

seventh (제칠)
che-ch'il

eighth (제팔)
che-p'al

ninth (제구)
che-gu

tenth (제십)
che-ship

(2) Fractions and Quantities

a half ____
____ 의 반
eui pan

half a ____
____ 반개
pangae

a quarter
사분의 일
sabun-eui il

three-quarters
사분의 삼
sabun-eui sam

a third
삼분의 일
sambun-eui il

a cup of ____
한잔의 ____
hanjan-eui

a dozen of ____
____ 한타스
han taseu

a kilogram of ____
일킬로그람의 ____
ilk'illogeurameui

a liter of
일리터의
il-lit'eo-eui

a little bit of ____
조금의 ____
choguem-eui

a lot of
많은
man-eun

a pair of ____
한 쌍의 ____
hanssang-eui

enough of ___
___충분한
ch'ungbunhan

too much of ___
너무나 많은___
neomuna man-eun

ratio
비례
birye

percent
백분의
p'aekbun-eui

twenty percent
이십퍼센트
ishipp'eosenteu

seventy percent
칠십퍼센트
ch'ilship-p'eosenteu

times as much
배
bae

six times as much
여섯배
yeoseot-bae

one hundred times as much
백배
paekbae

(3) Counting various things

o'clock   시   shi
한시 han-shi,   두시 tushi,   세시 se-shi

hour   시간   shigan
한시간 han-shigan, 두시간 tushigan,
세시간 se-shigan

time 번 beon
한번 han-beon, 두번 tu-beon, 세번 sebeon

ages 살 sal
한살 han-sal, 두살 tu-sal, 세살 se-sal

packs 갑 gap
한갑 han-gap, 두갑 tu-gap, 세갑 se-gap

man 사람 saram
한사람 han-saram, 두사람 tu-saram,
세사람 se-saram

animals 마리 mari
한마리 hanmari, 두마리 tu-mari,
세마리 se-mari

bound objects such as books, notebooks, and so
forth 권 gweon
한권 han-gweon, 두권 tu-gweon,
세권 se-gweon

houses 채 ch'ae
한채 han-ch'ae, 두채 tu-ch'ae, 세채 sech'ae

vehicles 대 dae
한대 handae, 두대 tu-dae, 세대 se-dae

bottle   병   byeong
   한병 han-byeong, 두병 tu-byeong,
세병 se-byeong

items   개   gae
   한개 han-gae, 두개 tu-gae, 세개 se-gae

small sticks such as pencil, brush, etc 자루 jaru
   한자루 han-jaru, 두자루 tu-jaru,
세자루 se-jaru

month   달   dal
   한달 han-dal, 두달 tu-dal, 세달 se-dal

sheets or tickets   장   jang
   한장 han-jang, 두장 tu-jang, 세장 se-jang

liquid(glasses or cups of.)   잔   jan
   한잔 han-jan 두잔 tu-jan, 세잔 se-jan

pairs of things to wear on feet or legs
   켤레   k'yeolle
   한켤레 han-k'yeolle, 두켤레 tu-k'yeolle,
세켤레 se-k'yeolle

suits(of clothes) 벌 beol
한벌 han-beol, 두벌 tu-beol, 세벌 se-beol

a pair, a couple 쌍 se-ssang
한쌍 han-ssang, 두쌍 tu-ssang,
세쌍 se-ssang

bowels 그릇 greut
한그릇 han-greut, 두그릇 tu-greut,
세그릇 se-greut

dishes 접시 jeopshi
한접시 han-jeopshi, 두접시 tu-jeopshi,
세접시 se-jeopshi

(4) Years and Counting Days

1900 (천구백년)
ch'eon gubaeng-nyeon

1988 (천구백팔십팔년)
ch'eon gubaeg-p'alship p'al-
nyeon

1990 (천구백구십년)
ch'eon gubaeg-kushim
-nyeon

1991 (천구백구십일년)
ch'eon gubaeg-kushib-il
-nyeon

one day	하루	haru	일일	ir-il
two days	이틀	it'eul	이일	i-il
three days	사흘	saheul	삼일	sam-il
four days	나흘	naheul	사일	sa-il
five days	닷새	tassae	오일	o-il
six days	엿새	yeossae	육일	yug-il
seven days	이레	ire	칠일	ch'ir-il
eight days	여드레	yeodeure	팔일	p'ar-il
nine days	아흐레	aheure	구일	ku-il
ten days	열흘	yeorheul	십일	shib-il
eleven days	열하루	yeol-haru	십일일	shibir-il
twelve days	열이틀	yeol-it'eul	십이일	shibi-il

(5) Counters Using Numberals

mimutes 분 bun
   일분 il-bun, 이분 i-bun, 삼분 sam-bun,
   사분 sa-bun, 오분 o-bun

years 년 nyeon
   일년 il-nyeon, 이년 i-nyeon, 삼년 sam-nyeon,
   사년 sa-nyeon, 오년 o-nyeon

won(Korean money) 원 won
   일원 ir-won, 이원 i-won, 삼원 sam-won,
   사원 sa-won, 오원 o-won

ages   세   se
일세 il-se, 이세 i-se, 삼세 sam-se, 사세 sa-se,
오세 o-se

floors or stories of building   층   ch'eung
일층 il-ch'eung, 이층 i-cheung, 삼층 sam-ch'eung,
사층 sa-ch'eung, 오층 o-ch'eung

serving portion   인분   inbun
일인분 ir-inbun, 이인분 i-inbun, 삼인분 sam-inbun,
사인분 sa-inbun, 오인분 o-inbun

(6) Date

1st (일일)	2nd (이일)
ir-il	i-il
3rd (삼일)	4th (사일)
sam-il	sa-il
5th (오일)	6th(육일)
o-il	yug-il
7th (칠일)	8th (팔일)
ch'ir-il	p'ar-il
9th (구일)	10th (십일)
ku'il	ship-il

11th (십일일)
shib-ir-il

12th (십이일)
ship-i-il

13th (십삼일)
shipsam-il

14th (십사일)
shipsa-il

15th (십오일)
shibo-il

16th (십육일)
shimyug-il

17th (십칠일)
shipch'ir-il

18th (십팔일)
ship'ar-il

19th (십구일)
shipku-il

20th (이십일)
ishib-il

21th (이십일일)
ishib-iril

22nd (이십이일)
ishib-iil

23rd (이십삼일)
ishibsam-il

24th (이십사일)
ishibsa-il

25th (이십오일)
ishibo-il

26th (이십육일)
ishibyug-il

27th (이십칠일)
ishipch'ir-il

28th (이십팔일)
ishibp'ar-il

29th (이십구일)   30th (삼십일)
ishibgu-il   samshib-il

31st (삼십일일)
samshibir-il

(7) Telling Time

A.M. (오전)   P.M (오후)
ojeon   ohu

noon (정오)   midnight (자정)
cheong-o   chajeong

o'clock (정각)
cheong-gak

koreans first say hours, next a list of minutes

1 o'clock (한시)   2 o'clock(두시)
han-shi   tu-shi

3 oclock (세시)   4 o'clock(네시)
se-shi   ne-shi

5 o'clock (다섯시)   6 o'clock (여섯시)
taseo-shi   yeoseo-shi

7 o'clock (일곱시)   8 o'clock (여덟시)
ilgop-shi   yeodeol-shi

9 o'clock (아홉시)
ahop-shi

10 o'clock(열시)
yeol-shi

11 o'clock(열한시)
yeolhan-shi

12 o'clock (열두시)
yeolttu-shi

1 minute(일분)
il-bun

2 minutes (이분)
i-bun

3 minutes (삼분)
sam-bun

4 minutes (사분)
sa-bun

5 minute (오분)
o-bun

6 minute (육분)
yuk-bun

7 minutes (칠분)
ch'il-bun

8 minutes (팔분)
p'al-bun

9 minutes (구분)
ku-bun

10 minutes (십분)
shib-bun

11 minutes (십일분)
shibil-bun

12 minutes (십이분)
shibi-bun

13 minutes (십삼분)
shibsam-bun

14 minutes (십사분)
shipsa-bun

15 minutes (십오분)
shibo-bun

16 minutes (십육분)
shibyuk-bun

17 minutes (십칠분)
shipch'il-bun

18 minutes (십팔분)
ship'al-bun

19 minutes(십구분)
shipku-bun

20 minutes (이십분)
ishib-bun

21 minutes (이십일분)
ishibil-bun

22 minutes (이십이분)
ishibi-bun

23 minutes (이십삼분)
ishibsam-bun

24 minutes (이십사분)
ishibsa-bun

25 minutes (이십오분)
ishibo-bun

26 minutes (이십육분)
ishimyug-bun

27 minutes (이십칠분)
ishibch'il-bun

28 minutes (이십팔분)
ishibp'al-bun

29 minutes (이십구분)
ishipku-bun

30 minutes (삼십분)
samship-bun

31 minutes (삼십일분)
samshibil-bun

32 minutes (삼십이분)
samshibi-bun

33 minutes (삼십삼분)
samshipsam-bun

34 minutes (삼십삼분)
samshipsa-bun

35 minutes (삼십오분)
samshibo-bun

36 minutes (삼십육분)
samshimnyuk-bun

37 minutes (삼십칠분)
samshipch'il-bun

38 minutes (삼십팔분)
samship'al-bun

39 minutes (삼십구분)
samshipku-bun

40 minutes (사십분)
saship-bun

41 minutes (사십일분)
sashibil-bun

42 minutes (사십이분)
sashibil-bun

43 minutes (사십삼분)
sashipsam-bun

44 minutes (사십사분)
sashipsa-bun

45 minutes (사십오분)
shshibo-bun

46 minutes (사십육분)
sashimnyuk-bun

47 minutes (사십칠분)
sashipch'il-bun

48 minutes (사십팔분)
saship'al-bun

49 minutes (사십구분)
sashibgu-bun

50 minutes (오십분)
oshib-bun

51 minutes (오십일분)
oshibil-bun

52 minutes (오십이분)
oshibi-bun

53 minutes (오십삼분)
oshipsam-bun

54 minutes (오십사분)
oshipsa-bun

55 minutes (오십오분)
oshibo-bun

56 minutes (오십육분)
oshimnyug-bun

57 minutes (오십칠분)
oshipch'il-bun

58 minutes (오십팔분)
oshipp'al-bun

59 minutes (오십구분)
oshipku-bun

60 minutes(육십분)
yukshib-bun

a quarter to two
두시 십오분전
tushi shibo-bunjeon

a quarter after two
두시 십오분 후
tushi shibo-bun-hu

2 : 15
두시 십오분
tusih shibo-bun-jeon

4 : 10
네시 십분
neshi shibun

6 : 30
여섯시 삼십분
yeoseotshi samsippun

(8) Various Months

two months ago (두달전)
tudal-jeon

last month (지난달)
chinan-dal

this month (이달)
i-dal

next month (다음달)
taeum-ttal

during the month of ____
____ 달 (동안에)
dal (dong-ane)

since the month of ____
____ 달 이후로
____ dal-ihuro

for the month of ____
____ 달에
____ dale

since the month of ____
____ 달 이후로
____ dal-ihuro

per month (한달에)
handale

one month (한달)
handal

a few months (몇달)
myeot-tal

PART V
TERMS FOR TOURING

(1) Airplane／Entrance

captain (기장)
kijang

stewardess (여자안내원)
yeojaannaeweon

cabin (객실)
kaekshil

seat number (좌석번호)
choaseokpeonho

boarding card (탑승권)
t'apsseunggueon

landing (착륙)
ch'angryug

take-off (이륙)
iryug

life jacket (구명대)
kumueongdae

blanket (모포)
mop'o

wet towel (물수건)
mulsugeon

pillow (베개)
begae

earphone (이어폰)
i-eop'on

disembark (상륙)
sangryuk

immigration (이민)
imin

terminal （터미널）
t'eomineol

passport （여권）
yeogweon

custom （세관）
segwan

baggage （수하물）
suhamul

flight number （항공편）
hang-gongp'yeon

transit （갈아타기）
karat'agi

quarantine （검역）
keomyeog

yellow card
예방접종증명서
yebangjeopjjongjeungmy-
eongseo

(2) Signs

entrance （입구）
ipkku

exit （출구）
ch'ulgu

no smoking （금연）
keumyeon

fasten seat-belt
좌석벨트착용
jwaseogbelteu-ch'agyong

transit （통과용）
t'onggwayong

call button （초인종）
ch'oinjong

waiting room （대합실）
taehapshil

danger （위험）
uiheom

for men (화장실)
hoajangshil

rest room (화장실)
hoajangshil

for ladies (여자화장실)
yeojahoajangshil

open (영업중)
yeong-eobjung

closed (폐점)
p'yejeom

trash (쓰레기통)
sseuregit'ong

information (안내소)
annaeso

keep out (출입금지)
ch'ulibgeumji

mail (우편)
up'yeon

(3) Hotel

front (후런트)
hureonteu

reservation (예약)
yeyak

room number (객실번호)
kaekshilbeonho

single room (1인용 방)
ilinyongbang

twin room (2인용 방)
iinyongbang

room with bath
욕실딸린 방
yokshilttalinbang

room without bath
(욕실없는 방)
yokshil-eomneunbang

information (안내소)
annaeso

suite(특별실)
teugbyeolshil

cloak room (짐보관소)
chimbogwanso

dining room (식당)
shikttang

lobby (대합실)
taehapshil

porter (짐꾼)
chimkkun

laundry service (세탁업)
set'ag-eop

hotel bill (계산서)
gyesanseo

bar (바)
pa

coffee shop (커피숍)
k'eop'ishop

(4) Dining

restaurant (식당)
shikttang

manager (지배인)
chibaein

assistant manager
(부지배인)
pujibaein

head waiter (급사장)
keubsajang

waiter (급사)
keupsa

chef (요리장)
yorijang

room rate(수박료)
sugbangryo

bill (계산서)
kyesanseo

menu (메뉴)
menyu

sanack bar (경양식당)
kyeongyangshikttang

cashier (회계원)
hoigyeweon

receipt (영수증)
yeongsujeung

fork (포크)
p'okeu

knife (나이프)
naip'eu

spoon (스푼)
sp'un

plate (접시)
cheopshi

glass (유리컵)
yurik'eob

table (식탁)
shikt'ag

ashtray (재떨이)
jetteori

soup (수프)
sup'eu

toast (토우스트)
t'ouseut'eu

butter (버터)
peot'eo

jam (잼)
chaem

fried egg (계란후라이)
kyeranhurai

medium (반숙)
pansug

ham (햄)
haem

vegetable soup
야채수우프
yach'aesup'eu

vegetable diet (채식)
ch'aesik

roast beef (로스트비프)
roseut'eubif'eu

fish (생선)
saengseon

tuna (참치)
ch'amch'i

bread (빵)
ppang

sandwich (샌드위치)
saendeu-wich

cheese (치즈)
ch'ijeu

beefsteak (비프스테익)
pip'seu'eik

boiled dgg (삶은 계란)
salmeun-gyeran

saussage (소시지)
soshiji

bacon (베이컨)
peik'eon

chicken (닭고기)
takkogi

omlet (오믈렛)
omulleteu

oister (굴)
kul

crab (게)
ge

cabbage (양배추)
yangbaech'u

carrot (당근)
tanggeun

onion (양파)
yangp'a

melon (멜론)
melon

grapes (포도)
p'odo

tangerine (귤)
gyul

salmon (연어)
yeon-eo

squid (오징어)
ojing-eo

lobster (왕새우)
oangsaeu

cucumber (오이)
oi

mushroom (버섯)
beoseot

spinach (시금치)
shigeumch'i

watermelon (수박)
subak

orange (오렌지)
orenji

pineapple (파인애플)
p'ainaepp'l

tomato (토마토)
t'omat'o

potato (감자)
kamja

eggplant (가지)
kaji

lettuce(상추)
sangch'u

celery (샐러리)
saelreori

apple (사과)
sagwa

strawberry (딸기)
ttalgi

peach (복숭아)
pogsung-a

banana (바나나)
panana

pear (배)
pae

(5) Drinking

beer (맥주)
maegjju

brandy (브렌디)
beurendi

whisky and soda
위스키소다
wiseuk'isoda

gin (진)
chin

gin tonic (진토닉)
chint'onig

cocktail (칵테일)
k'akt'eil

wine (포도주)
p'odoju

red wine (적포도주)
cheokp'ododju

white wine (백포도주)
paekp'odoju

champane (샴페인)
samp'ein

lemonade (레몬수)
remonsu

sugar (설탕)
seolt'ang

pepper (후추)
huch'u

juice (쥬스)
chyuseu

orange juice (오렌지쥬스)
orenjijyuseu

soy sauce (간장)
kanjang

salt (소금)
sogeum

water (물)
mul

hot water
뜨거운 물
tteugeo-un mul

sweet (단)
tan

bitter (쓴)
sseun

salty (짠)
jjan

sour (신)
shin

hot (매운)
maeun

(6) Transit

taxi (택시)
t'aekshi

automobile (자동차)
chadongch'a

bus (버스)
poeseu

rent a car (렌트카)
rent'euk'a

sightseeing bus
관광버스
kwan-gwangbeoseu

bus stop
버스정류장
beoseujeongryujang

railroad (철도)
ch'eoldo

train (기차)
kich'a

station (역)
yeok

sleeping car (침대차)
ch'imdaech'a

dining car (식당차)
shikdangch'a

subway (지하철)
chihach'eol

steamer (기선)
kiseon

road toll (통행요금)
t'onghaeng-yogeum

gas station (주유소)
chuyuso

parking (주차)
chuch'a

driver (운전기사)
unjeonmyeonheojeung

driver's license
운전면허증
unjeon-myeonheojeung

highway (고속도로)
kosokdoro

interchange (인터체인지)
int'eoch'einji

maximum speed
최고속도
ch'oigosogdo

minimum speed
최저속도
ch'oijeosogdo

ticket window
매표구
maep'yogu

one-way ticket
편도표
p'yeondop'yo

round trip ticket
왕복표
oangbokp'yo

(7) Sightseeing

sightseeing (관광)
kwan-gwang

reservation (예약)
ye-yak

cancellation (취소)
ch'uiso

itinery (여정)
yeojeong

harbor (항구)
hang-gu

river (강)
kang

waterfall (폭포)
p'okp'o

museum (박물관)
pangmulgwan

theater (극장)
keugjang

embassy (대사관)
taesagwan

library (도서관)
doseogwan

cathedral (사원)
saweon

garden (정원)
cheongweon

botanical garden (식물원)
shingmulweon

cable car (케이블카)
k'eibeulk'a

tour fare (여비)
yeobi

map (지도)
chido

admission fee (입장료)
ibjjangryo

guide (안내원)
annaeweon

mountain (산)
san

lake (호수)
hosu

landscape (경치)
kyeongch'i

art gallery (미술관)　　　　bank (은행)
misulgwan　　　　　　　　eunhaeng

consulate (영사관)　　　　park (공원)
yeongsagwan　　　　　　　kong-weon

pagoda (탑)　　　　　　　zoo (동물원)
t'ap　　　　　　　　　　　tongmulweon

hospital (병원)
pyeongweon

(8) Shopping

department store　　　　camera shop
백화점　　　　　　　　　사진기점
paekhoajeom　　　　　　　sajin-gijeom

duty-free shop　　　　　galssware
면세점　　　　　　　　　유리그릇
myeonsejeom　　　　　　　yurigeureut

optician's (안경점)　　　　shoe store (양화점)
angyeongjeom　　　　　　yanghoajeom

flower shop (꽃가게)　　　toy shop (골동품점)
kkokkage　　　　　　　　koldongp'umjeom

stationery (문방구점)
munbanggujeom

barber (이발소)
ibalso

beauty shop (미장원)
mijangweon

music store (악기점)
ag-gijeom

souvenir shop (토산품점)
t'osanp'umjeom

jewelry store (금방)
keumbang

tailor shop (양복점)
yangbogjeom

drugstore (약국)
yaggug

bookstore (서점)
seojeom

cosmetic shop (화장품점)
hoajangp'umjeom

chinaware (도자기)
tojagi

gold article (금제품)
kemjep'umjeom

silver article (은제품)
eunjep'um

cheap (싼)
ssan

ruby (루비)
rubi

sappire (사파이어)
sap'aieo

pearl (진주)
chinju

da-i-mond (다이아몬드)
da-i-amondeu

jade (비취)
pich'ui

fur (모피)
mop'i

leather (가죽)
kajug

purse (지갑)
chigab

necktie clasp
넥타이 핀
nekt'aip'in

wristwatch
손목시계
sonmokshigye

developing
필름현상
p'ileumhyeonsang

printing (인화)
inhoa

handbag (손가방)
son-gabang

discount(할인)
hal-in

expensive (비싼)
pissan

(9) Illness

hospital (병원)
pyeong weon

surgeon (외과의사)
oigwaeuisa

surgery (외과병원)
oigwabyeongweon

physician (내과의사)
naegwa-euisa

dentist (치과의사)
ch'igwaeuisa

nerse (간호원)
kanhoweon

specialist (전문의)
cheonmuneui

eye-doctor (안과의사)
angwaeuisa

first aid (응급치료실)
eunggeupch'iryoshil

bleeding (출혈)
ch'ulhyeol

pain (고통)
kot'ong

fever (열)
yeol

operation (수술)
susul

fracture (골절)
koljeol

chills (오한)
ohan

cough (기침)
kich'im

heart disease (심장병)
shimjangbyeong

headache (두통)
tut'ong

diabetes (당뇨병)
tangnyobyeong

stomachache (복통)
pokt'ong

insomnia (불면증)
pulmueonjeung

neuralgia (신경통)
shingyeongt'ong

eye drop （안약）
anyak

capsule （캡슐）
k'aepsyul

cotton wool （탈지면）
t'aljimyeon

prescription （처방전）
ch'eobangjeon

ointment （연고）
yeon-go

tablet （알약）
alyak

bandage （붕대）
bungdae

(10) Names of Government Agencies

The Blue House
청와대
ch'eongwadae

Prime minister's office
총리실
ch'ongrishil

Economic Planning Board
경제기획원 **
kyeongjegihoigwon

Ministry of Foregn Affairs
외무부 *
oimubu

Ministry of Domestic
Affairs   내무부*
naemubu

Ministry of Trade and In-
dustry상공부*
sang-gongbu

Ministry of Justice
법무부*
peommubu

Ministry of Information
공보부*
kongbobu

Ministry of Defence
국방부*
kukpangbu

Ministry of Energy and
Resources 동력자원부*
tongryeokjawonbu

Ministry of Agriculture
and Fisheries (농수산부*)
nongsusanbu

Ministry of Health and Social Affairs (보사부*)
posabu

Ministry of Communications
and Postal Services
체신부*
ch'eshinbu

Ministry of Sports
체육부*
ch'eyugbu

Ministry of Education
교육부*
kyoyugbu

Department of Taxation
국세청**
Kugsech'eong

Office of Immigration (출입국관리소**)
ch'ulibgukwaliso

The word for president is 대통령 (daet'ongryeong)
The word for Prime Minster is 총리 (ch'ongni)
To donote the head of each agency. add 장관
(changgwan' minster') to the words marked* and 장
(chandg head') to those marked**

(11) Names of Various Regions and Countries

United Nations (유엔)
yuen

Asia (아시아)
ashia

East Asia (동아시아)
tong-ashia

Southeast Asia
(동남아시아)
tongnam-ashia

South Asia (남아시아)
namashia

Europe (유럽)
yureop

Middle East (중동)
chungdong

North America (북미)
pungmi

South America (남미)
nammi

Central America(중남미)
chungnammi

Australia (호주)
hoju

New Zealand (뉴질란드)
nyujilandeu

phillipines (필리핀)
p'ilpp'in

Pacific region
(태평양지역)
t'aep'yeongyang jiyeog

Indonesia (인도네시아)
indoneshia

Malaysia (말레이지아)
maleijia

Singapore (싱가포르)
shingap'oreu

Thailand (태국)
t'aeguk

Taiwan (대만)
taeman

China (중국)
chung-guk

Hong Kong (홍콩)
hongk'ong

Japan (일본)
ilbon

U.S.A. (미국)
miguk

Canada (카나다)
k'anada

U.K. (영국)
yeong-guk

India (인도)
indo

Russia (러시아)
reoshia